GROWING UP

A Foot Soldier Looks Back

The Memoirs of a Vet of the 45th Division
(Thunderbirds) in World War II

By

Stanley E. Richardson

Introduction: George Garin

To my good friend
Chuck Malley ... in the
hope this will inspire
him to write about
his time in Alaska!

George

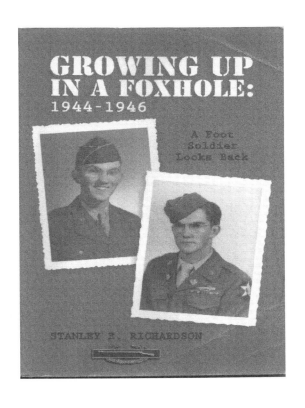

Front Cover of Original Edition

On the left Stan during his first month of basic training

On the right Stan 9 months later after his combat days

Original Cover Design: K.C. Kennedy

Healdsburg Frame & Graphic Design

ABOUT THE AUTHOR

After working at Massachusetts Institute of Technology after the war, Stan then worked under contract to the Atomic Energy Commission, later moving to the Environmental Protection Agency when it located in Montgomery, Alabama in 1972. Upon retirement, he and his wife, Chat, lived in rural, east Alabama.

Originally from New England, Stan enjoyed going back every year he was able to in order to visit family and friends. He stayed in touch with one of his war buddies throughout all the years. Stan passed away in November, 2012 in Alabama.

ACKNOWLEDGMENTS

I want to thank a former coworker, Mike Smith, who talked me into writing my memories of those days so long ago. I would be remiss if I didn't mention my cousin, Laurel Cook, an editor and author in her own right, who guided me along, almost page by page. Without her valuable assistance, I would long ago have given up this project.

DEDICATION

I dedicate this book to all the veterans who fought on the front lines in WWII and especially to those who gave up their lives so that we could live free. I also salute all the brave men of the 45th Infantry Division, the Thunderbirds, the combat infantry unit with which I served.

When you lose a friend you have an overpowering desire to go back home and yell in everybody's ear, "This guy was killed fighting for you. Don't forget him—ever. Keep him in your mind when you wake up in the morning and when you go to bed at night. Don't think of him as the statistic, which changes 38,788 casualties to 38,789. Think of him as a guy who wanted to live every bit as much as you do. Don't let him be just one of 'Our Brave Boys" from the old home town…"

From Bill Mauldin's *Up Front*

TABLE OF CONTENTS

INTRODUCTION

Although the invasion of Normandy in June 1944 and the Battle of the Bulge in December that year signaled the end of the war, we didn't know that at the time. When I signed up, it was thought that replacement ground troops would be needed for the battles ahead.

Most of the time we weren't told much; we just went from day to day. Once in a while, however, our platoon officer would tell us where we were and where we were headed. In other words, if the stories I tell here don't give you a history lesson, they are not meant to. It is one man's experience.

I did a lot of growing up in the two years I served with the 45th Infantry Division, and I know I was not alone in that. As I look back and retell it, I am constantly struck by how young we all were. We lost so many men in that war. The figures vary from 290,000 to over 400,000. Although it is referred to as "the good war," it is hard not to agree with the words of General William Tecumseh Sherman:

> You cannot qualify war in harsher
> terms than I will. War is cruelty, and

you cannot refine it; and those who brought war into our country deserve all the curses and maledictions a people can pour out. I know I had no hand in making this war, and I know I will make more sacrifices today than any of you to secure peace.

We did secure peace, and we went home to a grateful America, unlike veterans of later wars who deserved better. Somewhat like those who lived through the Holocaust and were reluctant to speak of those years to their children, we war veterans, while we might have told stories over a few beers, were also tight-lipped when it came to talking about the atrocities we saw and, worse, participated in. Some stories will never be told. It was a hard growing up, and equally hard to watch our own children come of age as eager as so many of us to sign up.

A psychologist said of war veterans suffering posttraumatic stress syndrome that, broadly speaking, you can divide them into two groups: those who cannot stand to think about their experiences and those who cannot stop thinking about them. And typically you see a mixture of these two. As WWII veterans are dying out, those of us who might have been tight-lipped for the past 60 years are opening up, trying to answer the questions their sons and grandchildren have, aware that we are, in a sense, living history.

We want future generations to see more than a textbook account of the war we fought so personally. We want them to see us, and also to get a glimpse of the "enemy," kids like us, as we recognize now. War now seems to be something that will always be with us. We don't seem to have learned anything from all the sacrifices made by millions of people the world over, time and time again. My father, Peter, fought in World War I, I fought in World War II and my son, George fought in Vietnam. What did we learn?

INTRODUCTION TO THIS NEW EDITION
BY GEORGE GARIN

I had the pleasure of knowing Stan Richardson for only a few months before he passed away in November, 2012. I had met Stan via an internet discussion group dedicated to the history of the 45th Division (Thunderbirds) in World War II. My father, who passed away at age 53 in 1975 after 30 years in the Army, had also served with the 180th Infantry Regiment of this fabled division.

Stan's emails always brightened my day. His humor and wisdom were remarkable, his responses always timely. I thoroughly enjoyed reading his Memoirs, clearly the memories of a humble and honorable representative of what so many have come to call the "Greatest Generation."

Stan and I did not limit ourselves solely to World War II matters. He shared with me some details of a second book about his life after the war that he was working on. I was helping him grapple with some of the niceties of computer program challenges he faced.

I'll copy and paste the last email I had from Stan below. I received it on Veterans Day in 2012 and responded immediately. I did not hear back from Stan the following day, as was usual. After waiting a few more days (and fearing the worst) I called his home in

Alabama. His daughter in law answered and confirmed my fears. Stan had suffered another heart attack and was in the hospital. However, he seemed to be recovering and was entertaining the nurses in the intensive care unit with his wit and charm. I asked Wendy to pass along my greetings and hoped to hear from Stan again once he had recovered. When, in early December I still had not heard anything more, I called again and this time got his wife, Chat. Chat shared the sad news with me that, after an initial period of improvement, Stan had relapsed and passed away. I had lost a cherished friend, one whom I was hoping to share much more with.

Knowing Stan had dealt with the dissemination of the wonderful, little book he had self-published, I eventually asked Chat whether I might ensure it would stay in print (both hard copy and electronically). Both she and Wendy were warm to the idea.

I have waited almost two years to follow through on that promise. It is a way for me to honor, not only Stan, but those countless others (like my dad) who were never able to share much of their World War II experiences. My hopes are that we and subsequent generations may learn from these honest depictions of the realities of war lessons that will aid us in the unending search for more peace and cooperation between nations and individuals.

I had not asked Stan to write anything specific in the copy of his book he sent me. He did inscribe it, however, with words that humble and challenge me. He wrote, "To the great Rev. Dr. George Garin." May this bit of work I have done to ensure Stan's book remains available to those wanting to know more help me live into that honor Stan so freely expressed.

The photo on the cover was taken about two months before Stan passed away. He was in Atlanta to receive, along with twelve other qualifying American Vets of World War II, the French Legion of Honor Medal at a ceremony at the French Consulate in Atlanta. The ceremony was an emotional time for Stan and an honor he deeply appreciated. Here was Stan's last email to me. He had simply copied and pasted a message for Veterans and Remembrance Day.:

It's Veteran's Day........!

<u>Remembrance Day</u>

He was getting old and paunchy
And his hair was falling fast,

And he sat around the Legion,
Telling stories of the past.

Of a war that he once fought in
And the deeds that he had done,
In his exploits with his buddies;
They were heroes, every one.

And tho' sometimes to his neighbours
His tales became a joke,
All his buddies listened quietly
For they knew whereof he spoke.

But we'll hear his tales no longer,
For old Bob has passed away,
And the world's a little poorer
For a Soldier died today.

He won't be mourned by many,
Just his children and his wife.
For he lived an ordinary,
Very quiet sort of life.

He held a job and raised a family,
Going quietly on his way;
And the world won't note his passing,
Tho' a Soldier died today.

When politicians leave this earth,
Their bodies lie in state.
While thousands note their passing,
And proclaim that they were great.

Papers tell of their life stories
From the time that they were young.
But the passing of a Soldier
Goes unnoticed, and unsung.

Is the greatest contribution
To the welfare of our land,
Someone who breaks his promise
And cons his fellow man?

Or the ordinary fellow
Who in times of war and strife,
Goes off to serve his country
And offers up his life?

The politician's stipend
And the style in which he lives,
Are often disproportionate,
To the service that he gives.

While the ordinary Soldier,
Who offered up his all,
Is paid off with a medal
And perhaps a pension - though small.

It is not the politicians
With their compromise and ploys,
Who won for us the freedom
That our country now enjoys.

Should you find yourself in danger,
With your enemies at hand,
Would you really want some cop-out,

With his ever waffling stand?

Or would you want a Soldier -
His home, his country, his kin,
Just a common Soldier,
Who would fight until the end?

He was just a common Soldier,
And his ranks are growing thin,
But his presence should remind us
We may need his like again.

For when countries are in conflict,
We find the Soldier's part,
Is to clean up all the troubles
That the politicians start.

If we cannot do him honour
While he's here to hear the praise,
Then at least let's give him homage
At the ending of his days.

Perhaps just a simple headline
In the paper that might say:
"OUR COUNTRY IS IN MOURNING,
A SOLDIER DIED TODAY."

CHAPTER 1: PEARL HARBOR

When the Japanese attacked Pearl Harbor on December 7, 1941, I was just a happy-go-lucky kid in my junior year in high school. I had just turned 15 years old and had no idea what the full impact of that event was going to have on me, my family and the rest of the world.

My stepfather and I were listening to the radio when President Roosevelt announced the attack on Pearl Harbor. I don't remember my stepfather having much to say about it in the moment, but I knew he had lived through World War I and had seen some of his friends go off to war, so I suppose he had some reaction he was covering up. I also knew that he hadn't been able to serve in World War I because of a leg injury he got as a teenager working in a coalmine in Illinois.

It was the day after Roosevelt shocked the country with the news that all the guys old enough to sign up for the service were scrambling to do just that. It didn't take long for cities and towns to form draft boards and register every available man for the war.

A lot of my classmates were already 17, even older, and although graduation was only five months away they were ready to quit school and enlist. Some did over the objections of their parents and some did with their parents' blessings—probably their father's. Mothers were not eager to see their sons go to war. As I recall, the Navy and the Marines would allow you to enlist at age 17 with or without parental consent. God, that seems so young today! For me, I stayed in school until I graduated in 1943. In the meantime, we read the newspapers, trying to stay abreast of what was going on.

At that time there was great secrecy about consignments, troop movements, and ongoing battles. We didn't have TV to bring the war into our living rooms. In those early years, the government gave a little white banner with a gold star embroidered on it to families that lost a son in the war. Most people hung it in a window for all to see. We had a few Gold Star families on my street. I had known some of them, and I remember trying to imagine what the parents must have gone through when they got the news that their son had been killed. We guys never talked about it. Up until that time, some of us may have gone to a wake or two when a father or mother died, but those folks were old and it didn't touch us that much. (We lived outside Boston in an area dominated by the Irish, and wakes were popular, if you can use that word. Some were pretty wild affairs involving a lot of drinking and story-telling that would go on for days.)

We had never known anyone in our age group that died and it was hard to comprehend the fact that someone we knew had been killed in some far-off place and we'd never see him again. (Sure, there was the kid, Ziggy, who dove into the Charles River from the foot bridge and fractured his skull. He walked around with bandages wrapped around his head like a turban, but he did live to tell the tale.)

It was customary in my neighborhood that when someone died the body was prepared by the undertaker and brought home for viewing. For a period of two or three days, friends of the deceased would come by to pay their respects. Although this practice, or similar rituals, may have survived among certain ethnic groups, most people in this day and age grimace at the thought of having a dead body, even a beloved member of the family, displayed in the front room. For us, the living room, or parlor, was used only for Sunday visitors or for wakes.

CHAPTER 2: FINALLY, MY TURN

I had been champing at the bit to join the service, and so as soon as I graduated from high school, I was off to the Marines recruiting station. I thought they were a great outfit. If you were a Marine, you got the respect of everybody.

I don't think I told my parents that I was trying to get into the Marines, but if they had put up any objections, I'm sure I would have enlisted anyway. That's how fired-up I was about serving in this war. As (bad) luck would have it, they wouldn't accept me because I wore glasses. I tried to join the Navy and was rejected for the same reason. I tried the Army Air Corps and, once again, I was rejected. I couldn't get into the Army, my last choice, because I was only 17 years old.

This really upset me. I wanted to serve my country in any branch I could. I didn't want to be labeled 4-F, as many were for things like flat feet, punctured ear drums, physical deformities, even having to wear glasses. A guy could look like a healthy specimen of manhood but if he was rejected and labeled 4-F he took a lot of verbal abuse from some servicemen, and even civilians I might add, who didn't know any better.

I was desperate to find a way to fool the Army Air Corps recruiting agent into accepting me in spite of my wearing glasses. I had discovered one day when I was kidding around making faces to get a laugh out of my cousin that if I crossed my eyes and covered one of them I could read without my glasses. It didn't make any difference which eye I covered. The only explanation I came up with is that perhaps a muscle was being forced into a position that caused the eye to come into focus. Anyway, it was worth a try.

Afraid that the recruiter I had gone to the first time might remember me, I made it a point to go to a different Army Air Corps recruiter for my next try. The recruiting office was in a large building that looked like a warehouse. The recruiter turned out to be a Master Sergeant who looked like one of my English teachers. He was a real friendly guy and I think he detected a bit of apprehension on my part. He told me to relax and then gave me some forms to fill out.

I had to take an IQ test before the physical. I passed that and then was called to take the eye test. The doctor asked me to take off my glasses and place them on his desk. He then gave me a card with some printing on it and asked me to cover my right eye and read the card. I covered my eye, crossed them and read the card. The doctor seemed surprised and asked me to read the card with my other eye. Now, I was very nervous. I covered my left eye, again crossing them to read the card, and, again, I did it.

He picked up my glasses, looked at them and said, "Read the card with both eyes open."

Well, he had me there; I couldn't make out the words at all. He was kind enough to smile and say I had made a nice try, and if I really wanted to get in the service, I'd probably have to wait until I was 18 and drafted.

Patriotism was running very high in those days and spirits were good. Everyone felt that we were going to win the war and everyone wanted to do their part. When I turned 18 in December of 1943, I had to register for the draft. At last I thought I'd be able to get into the service and do something for my country. Once again my eyes held me back. I was classified 1-AL which meant limited duty, but I kept after the draft board until finally, in August of 1944, they accepted me. I remember the sergeant at the recruiting office asking me, "Do you really want to go?" I replied, "Absolutely." Little did I know what I was in for.

Naturally, my folks were very upset. My stepfather said I'd be nothing but "gun fodder." I couldn't understand his worry until I became a parent myself and my son volunteered for duty in Vietnam when he turned 18. I had no inkling that he was going to do that. He almost brought tears to my eyes when he said, "Dad, you went in the Infantry when you were 18 and you came out okay." "Yeah," I said, "but I was awfully lucky." Then, I threw my arms around him and told him how proud of him I was. Inside, however, I felt as though I was going to lose him. Fortunately, he made it through with no serious wounds.

At 18 years old I had no idea that I would end up on the front lines fighting the enemy face-to-face. The day I left home, my folks wanted to go to the train station with me, but I wouldn't let them. I thought it would make me look like a little kid that needed to hold his Mama's hand. They were probably hurt, but they agreed to say goodbye at home. At last I was going to be in the service. At 17 you were still referred to as a teenager but at 18, and wearing a uniform, you were suddenly a man in everyone's eyes. If I ever felt proud, I guess it was at this time.

CHAPTER 3: BASIC TRAINING

I was "processed" at Fort Devens in Ayer, Massachusetts and then sent to Camp Wheeler just outside of Macon, Georgia. Part of the processing at Devens involved getting shots for various diseases. One of the new inductees, who was rather large, passed out after his third shot and, as he fell, he hit his head on the corner of an iron post and fractured his skull! I heard later that he was discharged with only two days of total service time. What will he tell his grandchildren when they ask him what he did in the war?

After the processing was over we were put on a train to head for what was to be our "home away from home." Our destination was a secret. At the time, that was rather scary but it was also exciting. I don't know how many of us were on the troop train but it was probably a couple of hundred at least. Probably about 95% of the guys on the train had never been on one before, much less been out of state. I heard things like, "Aw, this'll be a snap," and "I sure would like to know where we're going," or "Do we get anything to eat on this train?" One kid said, "I didn't get a chance to call my folks; they'll worry about me.

Not being sure of exactly what we would be doing or if we would be able to "take it," there was some uneasiness on our part. The day we arrived at Camp Wheeler in Georgia, the temperature was almost 100 degrees, a muggy heat that none of us Yankees were used to. Among the guys in my coach was a big, tall blond, about 6'2" who looked like he'd be able to handle anything that came along, but first impressions are not always accurate. After we detrained at the camp, several miles outside of Macon, we were told to line up and wait for further orders. We were all perspiring freely and I know I wasn't alone in wishing there was some shade to stand in. After about ten minutes in this heat we heard a little commotion down the line. The big, tall blond had fainted. That was the day we found out that we were in an Advanced Infantry Training camp.

I was starting to question why I had been so eager to enlist. We were being yelled at, told to hurry it up, and to "at least *try* to look like soldiers." The noncommissioned officers (NCOs) were not as friendly as the recruiters we had met. I wondered if we were going to be treated like this every day.

The rest of the afternoon was spent in getting our bedroll, our uniforms and our footlockers and finding the barracks where we had been assigned to live for the next four months. The next day we learned how to make a bed (when you made your bunk in the morning, the cover had to be tight enough that you could bounce a coin on it), store things in a footlocker and hang clothes in a metal wall cabinet. (No more having your mother pick up after you.) All clothes had to be hung in the same order, facing the same way. Everyone's footlocker had to be placed so that they all lined up looking the same for inspection. When our platoon was to be inspected, we were to stand by our footlockers at attention and look straight ahead.

Sometimes the officer of the day would randomly check the barracks. If there was one little thing out of line, our sergeant would get his ass chewed out, and that meant we were all in deep trouble. As a result, we all kept an eye on each other to make sure we wouldn't have to face the sergeant's wrath.

I'd like to know who the general was that decided on the correct way to fold clothes, what direction and order to put them in, and all the other little things that drove us crazy. It took us a while to get used to following all these petty details, but any infraction of the rules meant we'd *all* have to fall to the floor and do 33 push-ups. Why 33 was a magic number, I have no idea to this day.

We were also shown what and how to pack our backpacks. Primarily, it was things you'd need on a long march: eating utensils, gas mask, clean underwear, a raincoat—which turned out to be useless. We soon found out that we'd perspire so much wearing it that no one did. Still, we had to carry it. We were issued a folding shovel that was about two to two and a half feet when extended. It was for digging foxholes, mainly, but it could also be used as a chopping tool. We attached our canteen and canteen cup to our belt.

Each of us was required to take a turn at KP. It meant getting up around 3:00 A.M. and reporting to the mess sergeant. We'd have to set up the tables in the mess hall and keep the pitchers of water filled with water, coffee or hot cocoa. After the men had eaten we'd scrub the tables and wash all the plates and utensils to get ready for the next meal. This usually took three or four hours, just in time for the next meal. We'd finish around 11:00 P.M.

Our time in the afternoons was spent learning how to take care of our weapons and getting acquainted with how the Army operates and what was expected of us as soldiers. We had the Articles of War read to us more often than I thought was necessary. I know I felt more like a prisoner when they got through telling us what we could and could not do.

On our first day we were awakened at 4:00 in the morning by the platoon sergeant yelling, "OK boys, let go your cocks, grab your socks, it ain't daylight but it's 4:00 o'clock." Even though I had never in my life gotten up at 4:00 o'clock in the morning, I had to admit that seeing the sunrise was a beautiful sight.

We heard the sergeant's early morning call for a couple of weeks until we started waking up on our own. Besides seeing the sunrise, a major reason to jump up in the morning was to be among the first to get into the latrine. (I was quickly picking up the vocabulary of army life.) With 60 men to a platoon the lines to the urinals, hoppers, shower stalls and sinks could get long. If you hadn't finished your business by the time Sarge showed up again, you were out of luck.

By five o'clock, the platoon had to line up outside the barracks. When the Sarge yelled "Fall out!" by God, you'd better be outside the barracks, lining up. When he yelled, "Fall in," we had to line up in formation, and it was to be the same formation every day. Knowing who was going to be beside you certainly made it easier.

It took us a while to reach the speed that Sarge wanted us to achieve. I know most of us thought at that time that we were pretty fast, but Sarge wasn't satisfied. He made us go back into the barracks, stand by our cots, and wait for the call to "fall out." We had to do it over and over again until he was satisfied.

Some guys on the second floor—I was one— would jump out the windows, some only partly dressed, and then scramble to line up in formation. He didn't care if we broke doors down or trampled each other; he wanted everyone out there when he yelled "fall out!" Later, we found out that the platoon sergeants had a running bet on whose platoon could fall out the fastest! We found out that we were one of the fastest he had ever had. After that he eased up on us in certain areas.

After getting dressed and having inspections, our day started around 5:00 A.M. with an hour of exercise. Then we would fall in for breakfast. After breakfast we had another three hours of exercising, which included doing duck walks, squatting down, hands on hips, and walking around the area in front of the barracks, a distance of about 800 feet. Again, doing 33 push-ups was something you were told to do just about every time you turned around. They meant to get us in shape and they sure were doing it. I couldn't take a step the first week without a muscle hurting me somewhere.

If you were underweight you added weight and if you were overweight you took it off. I went from a slim 140 pound to a fairly decent, well-filled-out 160 pounds. Some of the "fatties" had a real hard time because they were so soft. But others succeeded. I remember one kid from Connecticut who came in at 240 pounds but finished basic training at a good solid 180 pounds. He said he hadn't felt that good at any time in his life. Living with 60 "men," a bunch of guys I had never met before, was quite an experience. The closest I ever came to it was when I was about 14 and my folks were able to send me to a YMCA camp for two weeks. There is a big, big difference, however, between a bunch of 14 year old boys and young men whose average age was 20.

They were from several different states and represented all sorts of backgrounds. Some came from extremely poor families, while a few had come from wealthy families. Some were barely educated and others were college students. Some were very shy and others were raunchy as hell. But somehow, we were able to form friendships in which one's background didn't matter. We were all in the same boat with a job to do. Within a couple of weeks, you'd think we had known each other all our lives.

In our 16 weeks of training we learned how to fire the M-1 rifle. We had to take it apart and put it back together again while blindfolded. (That was a skill I never had to use on the front lines.) We also learned to fire a 30-caliber machine gun, a 30-caliber carbine and the Army 45 pistol. I couldn't hit the broadside of a barn with the 45 but I did score "Expert" with the M-1, which I felt pretty good about since I had never fired a weapon before.

Some of the boys from Tennessee, Kentucky and Missouri who had grown up hunting deer, squirrels and rabbits did not fare as well as I thought they would. They posted scores only in the Marksman range. We also learned how to use a compass and read a map. After a while it sunk in that we were being taught the skills we would need not only to kill the enemy but to survive on our own.

We were really being pushed hard and it was cause for a lot of complaining, a euphemism for "bitchin'." You'd hear, "They're trying to kill us before we get outta here," "My legs are killin' me," "I'm thinkin' about goin' AWOL," and even "I should have listened to my mother."

Back in the barracks, we'd talk about what had gone on during the day. Most of us thought that a lot of what we were being taught would be of no use on the front line. "Logistics, tactics, strategies—that stuff is up to the officers, not us," one guy said, and everyone nodded. Actually, the night exercises that taught us how to move through the woods with no noise did help me more than once. After I got shipped overseas and became part of the 45th Infantry Division, only three weeks after I finished basic training, I had been on the front line a day or so when it was my turn to go out on night patrol.

I was told to sneak into enemy territory to see if I could find out anything. Talk about being scared! With my heart beating so hard that I thought sure the enemy would hear it, I did manage to slip past German sentries. Fortunately, I had very good vision at night. I still do.

I spotted a couple of German soldiers and a tank about 300 hundred yards in front of our position. The German soldiers were having a smoke and were walking down the snow-covered road towards me. In the wintertime, when the snow covers the ground and the tree branches, the night takes on a strange eeriness. I was behind a fairly large tree when the two soldiers stopped right in front of me. They were talking about something, who knows what, and had no idea I was there.

I stood with my back against a tree, facing away from them. I was breathing through my mouth because I didn't want them to hear me. I knew that when I breathed through my nose, I made a very slight breathing noise. I can breathe a lot faster with my mouth side open, and did it silently.

After what seemed like an eternity, they started walking back to the tank. In spite of the freezing cold night I was sweating bullets, as they say, as scared as I've ever been. I didn't think I was going to get back to my platoon. When I returned with my report the lieutenant said, "Boy, I didn't expect to see you again." That scared the hell out of me, also.

While I was in the service my basic pay was $50 a month plus $10 a month for being overseas and the whopping sum of $10 a month for combat pay! I would have gladly given up that $10 for combat if I thought I could. However, I did return literally unscathed for which I am forever thankful.

We had a night exercise in basic training where the task was to work our way through the woods without being seen or heard by "enemy" forces. "Spider" (his last name was Webb) apparently couldn't see in the darkness and walked off a 20-foot cliff. It was while he was in the hospital that they determined he had night blindness. I had never heard of night blindness but, looking back, I think my uncle might have had it. I remember being in the car with him as he drove over curbs, hit big potholes, and seemed to be oblivious to road conditions. I never thought about him not being able to see at night. I just thought he was a lousy driver.

Spider had been a college student when he got drafted so they gave him the option of remaining in the service with a desk job or getting an honorable discharge and going back to school. He chose the discharge.

I never walked off a cliff, but I did get hurt once on a training exercise. We were to run across an open field to engage the "enemy" in battle. Because the enemy was presumably firing at us, we had to run a zigzag course and dive for cover when we came upon a bush or some small shrub to hide behind. Well, I dove for a bush and got my foot caught under an exposed root. I called for one of my buddies to tell

Sarge that I was hurt. When he returned he told me that Sarge had told him to get me back to the barracks. He and another fellow more or less carried me back and put me on my cot and then left after notifying the company medic. When he came in to see me, he said I had a sprained leg and to stay off it for a couple of days.

This little misfortune happened in the 13th week of basic. That was a real problem, because if you couldn't go through the entire 16-week program, you had to repeat the whole thing. That was something I really did not want to do. I asked a few of my buddies to cover for me, if they could, without getting into trouble themselves. They said they would. One of them would answer "here" when my name was called at roll-call. Sarge went along with it, so I felt pretty safe about missing a couple of days' training.

The next morning my leg had swollen quite a bit. When I heard the medic coming upstairs to check on me, I dived under my bunk as fast as I had dived under the bush. He didn't see me; he probably thought that I had recovered and gone back to the platoon. It took about four days before the swelling went down enough that I could carry on. All that time, I stayed in the barracks and snacked on the food that some of the guys brought me from breakfast. My platoon would be gone all day, every day, so they made sure I had enough to eat.

Some of my memories of those early days are pretty funny. Still clear in my mind is a young kid from Connecticut. Only 5'2" tall, his nickname, as you might have guessed, was "Shorty." But it turned out that Shorty had a tally-whacker that was about eight inches long at rest. He was extremely self-conscious about it in his first week in camp. We knew because in the morning when we rushed to the latrine to be among the first to take a shower, Shorty was always the winner.

Most guys ran down naked while others had a towel around them. But with Shorty, even with a towel, you could see the tip of his you-know-what hanging in sight. After a week of good-natured ribbing, Shorty lost his shyness as he realized that, although he was short, he was a giant in the eyes of the guys in the barracks. With newfound confidence, he would strut down to the showers in the morning, swinging his tally-whacker for all to see, saying, "Eat your hearts out guys."

The talk of the barracks for a while was the time when the NCO assigned to instruct us on some military aspect of the Army didn't show up for our class. Instead we were introduced to a new NCO and told that he would be our instructor. We didn't think much about it, but later the word came down that our previous instructor had been caught "sleeping with" another NCO. I had never met a gay person, and most of us were surprised that he had made it into the

Army in the first place. The incident was soon forgotten.

Some problems we were given in our training exercises required making decisions based on what we had been taught, decisions that could mean life or death in combat. Up until that time, probably the only decision I ever had to make was whom I wanted on my side in a touch football game.

When you are in actual combat and you get an order to do something, you do it without thinking about it. You can go through the obstacle course in basic training where they use real ammunition but it's not the same as when you know that the enemy is *really* trying to kill you. But, far worse, no training exercise can prepare you for the helplessness you feel when you see a buddy get shot and hear him calling for help and you can't get out to him and pull him to safety. It's something you never forget.

Growing up in Cambridge, Massachusetts, I had never been to the South, but when you're in the service, you could be anywhere. I did have my eyes opened one Sunday, however, when I went to the Rec Hall, looking for something to do. A couple of guys were standing at the jukebox looking over the selection of songs. I joined them, but didn't see a single song that I recognized. I was a "Big Band" fan—Glen Miller, Tommy Dorsey, Charlie Barnet—and all I could see were "hillbilly" songs.

One of the guys said, "Well, it *is* Sunday. Maybe we should play a holy song." He punched the number for a song called "Wreck on the Highway." As I listened, I caught a line that said something like "there was a wreck on the highway, but nobody prayed." I don't know if he thought that was a "holy" song or if he was pulling my leg.

In Cambridge, the Black population lived in an area that covered about four or five city blocks located about a half mile from Central Square, the heart of the city. The schools were integrated and I was accustomed to being in classes with Blacks. The Southern states hadn't allowed integration—something I learned my first day in Macon.

But I was in for more surprises than segregated schools. One Saturday my buddy and I, after walking around the town, were waiting for a local bus back to the base. When the bus pulled up, without thinking I stepped aside to let a woman go first, something my mother had taught me. My mother had never been in the South and didn't know that her rules didn't apply to Black women in Macon, Georgia. A strange look came over the woman's face; I didn't know what to make of it. My buddy—I think he was from Tennessee—said quietly, "We get on first." I then noticed that the Blacks were the last to board the bus and that they all went to the back. It was quite an experience for me. Rosa Parks' refusal to go to the back of the bus was years in the future.

On later occasions when I went into town I saw that if a Black person was approaching whites on the sidewalk, he or she stepped out of the way to let them pass. If there wasn't enough room, the Blacks would step off into the street.

The Red Cross and Salvation Army had halls in Macon where we could go for coffee and donuts. The Red Cross charged us but the Salvation Army gave those things to us free of charge. The Red Cross got a bad reputation in World War II, and it was things like that that did it. The Salvation Army had a container by the door with a small sign inviting "any donation." It was a good psychological ploy because the GIs probably put more money in that container than the Red Cross was charging us. When the war ended in Europe and we were coming back through Camp St. Louis north of Paris, the Red Cross showed up and had the nerve to charge us for gum and candy. Most of the GIs told them what to do with their candy and gum.

Toward the end of basic training, a Corporal MacArthur was assigned to our battalion. He was arrogant, pompous and a real pain in the ass. He insulted us constantly—belittled our attempts at doing exercise and repeatedly reminded us that he was a corporal and we were only privates. These days you would say he needed an "attitude adjustment." About a week before we finished our training he asked for a transfer from our group and received it.

Rumor had it that he found a note on his bunk saying he'd better learn to swim with a crankshaft around his neck if he got shipped out with us. By this time I knew there were guys who wouldn't hesitate a second to throw somebody overboard if they felt he had it coming. At least we didn't have to put up with him anymore.

CHAPTER 4: FROM BASIC TO BATTLE

What I learned in basic training was more about myself than about fighting the enemy. I found out that I could go for 24 hours or more without sleep; I could crawl through mud and sleep out in the rain; I could make critical decisions when I had to; I could take over a squad and give orders; I could lead a bunch of guys and, most of all, I discovered I was a lot tougher than I thought I was. I'm probably not alone in realizing that had I been told beforehand what I was expected to do, I would have said, "you're kidding."

We finished training around the 21st of December, 1944, and you never saw a bunch of happier GIs. Before leaving on our seven-day pass to celebrate Christmas at home, we had to have our pictures taken. I didn't like to have my picture taken, but now I'm glad I did. After all, we'd be going overseas and though the thought never entered my head, the families surely knew that we might not come back.

In those days civilians were bumped from the trains to give servicemen the seats. Because snowstorms around Maryland and New York those headed north were held up a couple of days. I ended up having only four days at home before I had to report back to a camp in Maryland. I wanted to make the most of my time.

When I got home and walked in the door, I felt as though I had really accomplished something. I was not their little boy anymore. We gathered in the living room and I had to answer a million questions. "How did you like it?" "Were you scared?" "Did you miss us?" "Where are you going from here?" I stayed home that night and had a meal that only my mother could have prepared. She cooked everything I liked.

The next day I made a few calls to see if any of my friends were home. I found a couple and set up a time when we could get together. I ran into some of my buddies who hadn't been able to get into the service. They seemed to be embarrassed about it, although it wasn't mentioned.

Most of the guys on my street had joined the Navy and one had managed to get into the Army Air Corps. Some of them ended up with nice, easy jobs. One spent two years stationed in Apalachicola, Florida, packing parachutes. He was 1,350 miles from home the whole time, but I think he managed to get a leave at least once a month.

In minutes, it seemed, it was time to leave again. I arrived at a camp in Maryland for further processing prior to going overseas. The good news is that before shipping out we were given a pass that allowed us to go into town for the evening. The social director at the camp told us there was a girls' college in town that held parties with a standing invitation to any soldier in camp. That was all we needed to hear. I think there were about six of us that took the bus into town. Talk about a bunch of GIs getting excited, man, we were ready to go.

I went to one party that was held in a big hall. It was a GI's dream come true. The night could have lasted forever as far as we were concerned. We danced and danced and I guess it was a good thing that there were no alcoholic drinks being served or some of us might have gotten into trouble.

We all got offers for dates with these girls for the coming weekend. We were on Cloud Nine the rest of the night. The next morning was the shocker: we would be shipping out that afternoon. We couldn't call the girls to tell them we wouldn't see them again. Our morale sure took a beating that day.

Our orders called for us to be on one of the piers of New York City where we would board a ship. I had been to Greenwich Village once in the summer of 1941 to visit an uncle who lived on West 8th Street. It was alive with people of all ethnic groups. I remember listening to street musicians and singers— pop to operatic—and stopping to watch jugglers and acrobats performing on the sidewalks. The Village was, and is still, where artists and writers want to be.

On this trip, however, we didn't know where we were going, just that we were on our way to the front lines someplace. Three weeks later, in the middle of winter, I was in France in a snow-covered foxhole that was to be my new home.

We arrived in New York City aboard a troop train around midnight. It was so dark, it was difficult to see just how many of us were there on the pier. Having lights on had been a no-no since the early days of the war. The whole country had to observe the blackout rules. No lights could show from any house or building after dark. Automobiles, if permitted to travel at night had to have most of their headlights taped up with only enough light showing to be seen by other motorists.

I didn't see anybody I knew that had been with me in basic training. Whoever was in charge of troop movements sure knew what he was doing. Every one of us was assigned to a place aboard ship before we even got on it. I was told later that we had about 15,000 GIs on board so they must have been loading quite a while before we arrived.

The ship was the *Queen Elizabeth*, the biggest liner afloat. A more somber group you wouldn't find anywhere. Finally, we were told to start up the gangplank. An Army band played, "Empty Saddles in the Old Corral." I suppose there was a sexual implication there that someone thought was funny but I didn't see anyone laughing.

I was surprised at how soon the ship started to move out of the harbor. Although we would be passing the Statue of Liberty, no one was allowed on deck. It was a sight reversed for those who made it back, and it had a lot more impact then, anyway.

The *Queen Elizabeth* is no small ship, but we were packed in like sardines. The compartment I was in had five or six folding bunks lining the walls, one above the other, with 18 inches or so between each one. Almost 60 people were crammed into a space 24 feet by 14 feet. The other compartments held as many or more.

I don't remember what deck I was on but we ate down on "G" deck, which felt like it was a hundred feet below sea level. I think we all found it depressing, being herded about like a bunch of cattle, still not knowing where we were going, not knowing anybody, and left standing around all day with nothing to do. We managed to occupy our time by sunning ourselves on the deck or reading, or gambling, much like rich old duffers on a cruise. The favorite game was craps. There were so many games going on I couldn't count them all.

A GI would set up a blanket on the deck. He was in charge of the game and kept it honest. He decided whether or not the dice had been rolled correctly, and his word was always honored. He would get 10% of any winnings a GI made. Sometimes an offer would be made by another GI to "buy" the blanket so he could make some money. After a few hours of running a game the owner would usually sell out to anyone who wanted to buy the spot for a reasonable profit.

There were so many GIs around a game that I never got close enough to actually roll the dice myself. Some of us would ask what the point was and we'd bet with others on the outside of the group actually shooting. With this side-betting I did make a few dollars.

As for reading, *Forever Amber* was the hottest thing around. By the time it got to me, it was in sad condition, but that didn't keep me from thoroughly enjoying it. Most of us hadn't read bestsellers with that much sexual content. I since found out that its author, Kathleen Winsor, died in 2003 at the age of 83.

Guys started getting seasick as soon as we got out in the open sea. One kid stayed in his bunk for five days. We brought him candy bars and crackers to eat; those were the only things he could keep down. The crew had set up big 55-gallon drums about every hundred feet so that we were never far from a place to upchuck. It was not uncommon to see guys who

[47]

couldn't get to the drums hanging over the rail. I don't know who was responsible for emptying the drums but it was probably the worst detail a crewman could have.

I thought I was going to escape being sick, but on the third day out I joined the rest of them around one of those drums. It started at breakfast time. We had gone down to G deck, formed our chow line and picked up our eating utensils. Oatmeal, thick and heavy, was all I remember seeing on the steam tables that morning. The cooks ladled out a couple of spoonfuls and dropped them into our bowls. For milk, we didn't get more than two or three tablespoons, not enough to thin out the "goop."

I tried to eat as much as I could just to keep from being hungry. I had taken maybe three or four mouthfuls when I got the sensation that the oatmeal I had just downed was coming up to meet me. I broke out in a cold sweat and realized that if I didn't get out on the deck in a hurry, some of the guys around me would be in for a nasty surprise. I immediately headed for the first barrel I saw. Never having been seasick before, I appreciated what the other guys had been going through. Luckily, I was sick for only a day. It was the same when I returned home on the *Aquitania*. The third day out of England and there I was, keeping company with the big blue barrel.

The *Aquitania*, I've been told, also served in World War I. This voyage in 1945 was to be its last. There were times that we were sure the ship wouldn't make it back to the States. It rattled and shook and scared a lot of us with the noises she made. Whenever the ship went over some large swells, the twin propellers would come up out of the water a little bit. Then the ship would really start to shudder and shake.

It's funny now, but at the time we weren't laughing. Especially me. I was sitting in the head during one of these swells when the ship nearly shook me off the seat. Talk about being scared. I remember thinking that I sure didn't want to be someone who survived the war only to die in the open sea when an old ship on its last voyage went down in the middle of nowhere.

CHAPTER 5: OUT TO SEA

As we pulled out of the dock that night in January 1945, the buzz was that we'd be taking a route to Europe that the German U-boats didn't usually follow. If they were spotted, "we'll just outrun them." Hah! That was probably just to make us feel better.

With the seasickness behind us, we had a half decent trip. After six days of good weather, we landed in Grenoch, Scotland, again in the dark of night. At the time, we had no idea where we were. We were hustled off to waiting troop trains. By morning we were in England. From there it was a fast trip on a large Army vessel across the English Channel to Le Havre, France. We were standing out on deck when we had our first look at the bombed-out city. You could see clear across the city because there weren't any building left to block the view. It was sobering to see the extent of the destruction.

As we were debarking, a sergeant on the dock was asking if anyone played a musical instrument. It seems he had authorization to "draft" musicians out of the Infantry into an Army band. He managed to get two or three volunteers so I imagine their days as a "dogface" (any combat man) came to an end before they ever fired a shot. As eager as I had been to enlist, by now I found myself wishing I had learned to play something.

[50]

We were broken down into groups of varying sizes to be shipped up to the front lines as replacements. Once again, we were on a troop train and packed in like sardines. I was so cramped in my seat I thought I'd just stretch out under the seat. I managed to get down on the floor, turn my feet sideways and ease them under the seat across from me. When I lay down I had to turn my head sideways to get it under the seat. For a few seconds, it felt great to be able to stretch out, but all of a sudden I felt trapped and broke out in a cold sweat. I hadn't known I was claustrophobic. I worked my way back out and got into my seat again.

We were all strangers on the train because we hadn't been shipped out as a unit from a particular training camp. Still, it didn't take long for us to get to know each other. The trip to the Replacement Depot was only a few hours, though, so our beginning friendships ended abruptly. We did share one incident that scared us all for a while. The train was strafed by a German fighter plane. As far as I know, there were no injuries.

We had a layover in a small French town for about 20 minutes. There were several civilians who came up to the windows to talk to us. I had three years of French in high school but I couldn't understand a word they were saying. We offered them candy bars and cigarettes in return for bread.

I remember one bearded fellow we were trying to communicate with by repeating the word, "pain" for bread. He shocked us all when he said in perfect English, "knock it off guys, I don't have any bread but I would like some cigarettes." It turned out that he'd gone AWOL from some outfit and had been hiding out in this small village. I don't know if he ever returned to the States. How would he explain it? I suppose he could say he was captured by the Germans and managed to escape.

After arriving at the "Repo Depo"—it was now about ten days since we had left our families in the States—we were assigned to various units and given directions on how to find our unit. I was 2nd platoon, Company I, 180th Infantry Battalion, 45th Infantry Division. This division was known as the Thunderbirds. Their insignia is the stylized golden eagle in a field of red.

I don't remember how far I walked that night to join my outfit but it wasn't too far. The road up to the front was covered with snow and the temperature was probably about 20 degrees. Being from New England, the cold didn't bother me that much. I finally met someone who led me off into the woods. It was very dark and I couldn't make out the faces of those I met. I was introduced to the guy whose foxhole I would share. You'd think I would remember his name, but I don't. The Foxhole was just big enough for two.

All the guys now had beards and long hair. Nobody shaved; the whiskers helped keep the face a little warmer during winter months. About a month after I arrived on the front lines, I had a beard also. When we were finally pulled off line and got a chance to shave, the only way I recognized these guys was by their voices. They looked so much younger than I thought they were. I guess the average age was about 20. I had just turned 19 four weeks before I arrived in France.

Most foxholes were made to hold two GIs. Maybe the thinking was that an extra body provided a little more heat at night. I was glad that this guy had already dug a foxhole big enough for two before I got there. He must have had faith that he would soon have a foxhole buddy, or else he liked to stretch out at night.

Digging foxholes, oddly enough, gave us something to do during the cold winter days. When you are in snow two feet deep, you first had to clear away an area that would accommodate a hole big enough for two. Being in the woods made digging extremely difficult because invariably you would hit a tree root.

Once you determined that the hole was big enough to lie down in, roomy enough to turn over with a guy next to you, and deep enough to sit up in, you were ready to spruce it up. You gathered up pine boughs to line the bottom. Then you covered the boughs with a shelter-half (one half of the canvas tent we carried in our knapsacks) and used large branches to cover the top of the hole. The second shelter-half (supplied by your buddy) was placed over the branches. Snow had to be shoveled on top of that. Then, you cut one corner of the hole so you could leave without disturbing the top.

We also cut a shelf in the side of the hole to hold personal belongings, cookies and candy sent from home, and the two cans of beer included in our weekly rations. Guys like me who didn't drink beer usually found someone who would swap their candy for our beer ration. Believe it or not, it made a fairly snug place to sleep.

Our winter clothes consisted of anything we could get hold of to keep us warm. I wore long johns, a couple of shirts, a sweater, a field jacket and an overcoat. At night I would use my field jacket for a pillow and my overcoat for a blanket. I also wore a woolen cap under my helmet liner. My foxhole companion did the same. So it wasn't at night we worried about being cold, it was standing around all day in the snow with nothing to do that froze our butts off—and our feet!

I wore two pairs of socks, which helped some, but my feet were always cold. Everyone had cold feet--brave men, yes, but lots of cold feet. I think my toes came close to being frostbitten; they bothered me for a few years after I got out of the service, mainly when the cold weather approached.

Even the Shoe-Pacs we were given left a lot to be desired. They looked good, and felt warm and comfortable to start with. After a while, however, your feet would start getting cold again. I remember that my feet would start to sweat and then the sweat would start to freeze. The insulation was not as good as we thought it would be so there wasn't much to be gained from wearing them, although I am sure the Army meant well when they purchased Shoe-Pacs for the troops. I know that GIs in Korea had a bad time in the winter with these Shoe-Pacs and many did lose toes because of frozen feet.

In basic training we were told to take our boots off at night to give our feet some air and let them "breathe." I took mine off the first night I slept in the foxhole. In the morning my boots were frozen and I had to massage the hell out of them before I could get them on. After that I removed them only to massage my feet once or twice a day.

We carried a lot of stuff in our backpacks—mess kit, K rations (I usually kept one meal in a pocket of my field jacket), soap, toothpaste and brush, shelter half (one half of a tent), a blanket and extra socks. One of our most prized articles was toilet tissue. It came in a small pack, fan-folded, tannish-brown (good choice of color). Most of us were always on the lookout for extra packs and I think I was not alone in carrying some inside my helmet. It was the only place that stayed dry all the time.

I also carried two bandoliers of ammo for my M-1 rifle (about 5 or 6 clips to a bandolier, each clip holding eight rounds), two phosphorous grenades and two anti-personnel hand grenades. I carried the hand grenades in the straps on my chest but I carried the phosphorous grenades in the webbing strips on my back. I didn't want a bullet to hit me in front and cause one of those big ones to explode. It may not seem any better to carry the hand grenades on my chest but that's what most of us did. (Most GIs wouldn't carry the phosphorous grenades at all). I also carried my canteen and cup on my belt. I guess that we'd rather go out with a big bang than in a blaze of glory.

We used to write mail at night on the special lightweight paper the Army provided. By the light of a flame from a small beer bottle filled with gas, we were able to see enough to write. A small piece of rag was used for the wick. One drawback was the amount of black smoke produced by the burning gas. When we'd fall out in the morning, you could tell who had been writing by the soot around his nose and forehead.

I noticed that a lot of guys left their rifles leaning against a tree at night rather than keep them in the foxhole where it was dry. In basic training you were told over and over again: never let your rifle get dirty or rusty; our lives were going to be dependent on having one that would never fail. I asked one GI what he would do if the inside of the barrel got rusty. He said he'd just fire a round through it and it would be fine again. Apparently, that worked and it saved cleaning your rifle every day.

CHAPTER 6: WE SEE SOME ACTION

In Basic Training we had 60 men to a platoon, 12 men to a squad. I don't believe we ever had more than 24 to 26 guys in our platoon on the front line at any one time—and I remember well one night when we had only a few men.

About six rear-echelon members of an intelligence fact-finding unit appeared, wanting someone to escort them to a spot they had marked on their map as a good place for an outpost. I directed them to our platoon officer who made it clear that they were asking for trouble since most of the area they were looking at had not been taken yet. In the end, he relented and let them go, sending two volunteers to accompany them. He chose the volunteers by pointing and saying: "You and you, go with them." I was one of the "you" guys. I didn't want to escort these yo-yos but I had no choice.

My buddy, Jerry, and I couldn't believe our ears when their officer told them to shoulder arms and follow him. He said he had a good idea of how to get to this location, and he started off like he was on a Sunday stroll through a park somewhere. It was clear that these "intelligence" folks hadn't had any instructions on how to go through a section of countryside that could be harboring an unknown number of Germans. Surely, they must have had some basic infantry training before they arrived here. They should have known how to reconnoiter an area before risking their lives as well as those of others. You don't assume that there isn't anybody lying in wait for you. Even at night, you try to get a scout out and look around. Even without training, I would think that common sense would tell you to be very careful. Jerry and I had assumed that we would be sent out ahead of these guys to check things out, but no, we ended up following them. I think we even fell back a little so we wouldn't get caught by surprise if they were jumped on.

We got shot at once. I knew it was too dark for a German to see us so I figured he was just firing at a noise he heard. But Jerry and I hit the ground anyway. Another shot was fired and I saw a tracer (a bullet that leaves a luminous trail) hit his backpack. We got up after a minute or so and continued on. I don't think the officer and his men even slowed down. Eventually, the officer in charge told us that we had arrived at the hill he was looking for. He and his men were going up to a flat area, spread out, and dig foxholes and we were to do the same.

We got to the top of the hill but couldn't see anything in the dark. Now, ordinarily, we wouldn't bother digging a foxhole. There seemed to be enough trees to give us protection from enemy fire if it came. However, now knowing what may be in the area, and just to be on the safe side we decided we'd each dig us a little foxhole for some cover. In a situation like this, and from experience, we very seldom dug a hole deeper than a couple of inches.

We had no sooner started to dig when I heard a voice say, in German, "Hans, what's up." Even though we were trying to be very quiet, I guess he heard us as we started to dig. I think my heart stopped beating because the voice could not have been more than 20 feet away in the woods. I understood Hans to say "I don't know." It was too dark to see anything so we couldn't use our rifles, and the Germans were in the same boat. Jerry and I didn't move a muscle. My ears were straining for any sound that would tell me whether or not they were investigating the noise they heard. At the time I didn't think about it, but obviously they were just as scared as we were. We laid there for what seemed an eternity, until the sky started to get light. At least the officer and his men kept quiet until morning. We didn't see or hear anybody so we crawled around and found a couple of empty foxholes. The intelligence group found a few more.

As it turned out, we had crawled into the middle of a German outpost! Fortunately for us, they had dug their foxholes about 30 feet apart and in a circle about 60 to 70 feet in diameter. I would estimate there were probably six to eight Germans there. When they heard us they decided that since we were going to dig in ourselves there must have been a lot of us coming. Anyway, there weren't going to wait and find out.

Ironically, as much as I hadn't wanted to be a part of this escapade, it probably save my life and Jerry's. When we got back to our outfit the next day we found out that they had gone out on a patrol later the same night, and had walked into a minefield. Three or four had been killed and several wounded. By morning, we had only twelve men left in our platoon so we made up two squads of six each.

We had been advised in Basic Training not to get to chummy with our buddies because they may be killed or wounded and we wouldn't see them again. I guess they were trying to prevent emotional breakdowns, but you can't help but get attached to the guys you're with. When your life depends on someone else, as his does on you, you are going to feel the loss if one of them is suddenly wounded or killed. That's human nature. Everyone has read stories about GIs who fought side by side on the front lines and became lifelong friends, even though their time together was brief.

Down to so few men, we were probably high on the list to get some replacements, because it wasn't long before we had another squad. When we'd lose a few men, our commanding officer would get in touch with the Replacement Depot and request as many men as he could. Since other units also needed replacements we didn't always get the number of men we wanted. Sometimes we'd get anywhere from one to three spread over a few days' time. Even so, we were never able to maintain any real strength due to casualties.

We went through a lot of what we called "90-day wonders," mostly college students who had qualified for Officer Candidate Training. At the end of a three-month course they were given 2nd Lieutenant bars and became platoon leaders. I will give them a lot of credit, though, because they really tried to be good officers. Some were killed on the first day on the line while others were wounded badly enough to be sent to the rear for medical attention. Most of them asked for our advice and took what we had to offer, except for one that stands out in my mind.

It was an officer who wanted to reconnoiter the area ahead of us even though we told him what and who was out there. He wouldn't listen and told our sergeant to get a couple of riflemen because he wanted to see the area personally. Shouldering his carbine, he started out as if he were going for a Sunday stroll. He got about 100 yards ahead of the Sarge and his boys who were exercising extreme caution. How I would like to have seen the lieutenant's face when he found himself eyeballing the enemy that captured him. Fortunately, Sarge and boys were far enough back to avoid being seen. They were laughing their heads off when they got back and told us what happened. The lieutenant's total time with us was about two hours. After the war was over I heard that he had survived being a prisoner and was in pretty fair shape.

After all these years, that winter is mostly a blur. Only a couple of incidents remain clear to me. My folks had given me a wristwatch with a luminous dial when I graduated from high school. It came in very handy when we stood guard duty at night. Our time to stand guard duty depended on how many guys we had in our squad. Guard duty at night was usually about two hours long. You cannot imagine how long two hours can be when the temperature is close to zero and you feel like you're freezing to death, it's pitch black, and you swear that every twig falling through the branches is a German sneaking up on you!

The first man to stand watch didn't usually start until about 10:00 P.M. That left about seven or eight hours of darkness during the winter months. If we had six men in the squad that meant each man had to spend more than an hour on guard duty. My watch was passed from the one on guard to the next one on the list. Without fail, my watch would be anywhere from 20 minutes to almost an hour fast in the morning.

If you were the last one who stood guard in the morning you knew the watch had probably been moved up but you didn't know by how much. You did know that the day should be getting lighter by 5:30 A.M. and if it was still pitch black when the watch said it was 6:00 A.M. you knew you were going to stand longer than your allotted time.

Guard duty was no fun, let's say. Try to picture sleeping in a hole in the ground in the middle of winter; it's very cold outside, but you're fairly snug and warm in your foxhole. Depending on what shift you have to stand (after midnight each one is bad) you are awakened by the one who just finished his watch. Your name only had to be whispered and you were wide-awake and ready to take your position. You put on the clothes you may have taken off when you hit the sack, then lift the corner of the shelter-half and crawl out of the foxhole, trying not to disturb your buddy. The guard line, for our squad, was probably only 50 to 100 feet in front of us. You're all alone, in the cold and darkness, listening for anything that may be moving up on you. At first the cold doesn't seem all that bad, but after 15 minutes or so it starts to get to you. After all, you are mostly standing or sitting, not moving around very much.

It is so quiet you can almost hear your heart beating. Even a twig falling from a tree makes enough noise to get your attention. You never knew when it might be an enemy soldier out on night patrol, scouting the area or maybe a unit making an infiltration attempt. Under those conditions, an hour or two is a very long time. It's no wonder my watch was fast every morning.

[64]

Would you believe that the main reason we wanted to get some replacements was to cut down on the time we had to stand guard at night? Most of us felt we could face the enemy with just a few guys; what we really longed for was more sleep at night. Nobody could sack out in his foxhole during the day, although, believe it or not, if we had to, most of us could nod off just leaning against a tree. We were going on nerves most of the time.

The kitchen unit arrived around 6:00 in the morning, and that was our hot meal: thick oatmeal, very little milk to add to it, powdered eggs, hot coffee and maybe toast and jelly. The rest of our meals were K-rations. To this day, I will not eat Spam, and I'm probably not alone in that.

Although our main purpose on the front lines was to meet and overcome the enemy, we were always on the lookout for potatoes and bread to supplement our diet. Once in a great while we would find some eggs hidden in the overhead rafters in a cellar, behind dishes in a cabinet and just about any other place you could think of. We would promptly appropriate them. I remember one GI found a few eggs in the sewing basket of a woman who was still living in her house. I was beginning to think we looked harder for food than we did for German soldiers.

Once in a while we'd find a loaf of dark, rye bread. If we were really lucky, we'd find an egg or two. We knew there had to be a chicken or chickens somewhere but the owners were careful to hide them. One of the guys in my squad carried a frying pan he had found. When we were hungry we'd open a can of corned pork loaf, stick it in the pan and when all the grease was out of it, we'd throw the corned pork loaf away and fry up the potatoes or eggs. It was great.

Once we came across a warehouse loaded with furniture and various odds and ends. One GI found a large crock full of pickled eggs. I found a small box that had five cans of sardines in it. We both felt like we had struck gold. I immediately opened one can and devoured the contents. My plan was to ration myself—eat one can a day for the next four days. Then I thought, "Hell, I may be dead tomorrow," and I ate the rest of the sardines. When I think of it now, I have to scratch my head.

Most of the German families were having a difficult time themselves when it came to finding enough to eat. The retreating German soldiers took any food they could find so that they would have enough to eat themselves. As much as we scrounged around for food for ourselves, our troops were really compassionate when they came across a family that was literally starving. Without hesitation, these guys would share their K-rations with them, especially if there were young children. Many a German family, in spite of their fear of us, shed tears of gratitude when we gave them food.

[66]

One day we noticed a fellow GI limping up the snow-packed road. He said he was on his way back to headquarters because he had developed a severe case of athlete's foot. Some of us asked him how we could get it. Short of treason, we'd do almost anything to get off the front line. One GI actually asked him to take off one of his boots and sock so he could rub his foot against his. No dice. The fellow limped on his way.

After spending the winter on line we were finally replaced by another group. In all that time we never fired a shot. I guess the Germans were just as cold and miserable as we were but we didn't think about that.

One rumored incident made the rounds, though, and I think perhaps it is true. A group of German soldiers, mainly old men and teenagers, were trying to surrender to the Americans. As they came out of the woods with their hands raised above their heads, a German SS trooper opened fire on them, killing several and wounding a few. It was hard for us to imagine such a thing but we did know that the SS troopers were fanatics when it came to fighting for the Third Reich. By trying to surrender, the men, I suppose, were thought guilty of desertion, a serious offense for either side in any war.

As bad as things got for us, and as much as we talked about wishing we were someplace else, desertion was never an option for any of us. In fact, when a soldier was wounded and sent to the rear to a hospital to recuperate, it was always on his mind to rejoin his outfit as soon as they would let him. We knew guys to go AWOL from a hospital so they could rejoin their outfit and their buddies. Of course some of the guys they knew were no longer around because they, too, had been wounded or killed in action. The attachment to the outfit you were assigned was a very strong one. The bonds you formed with the guys fighting beside you is something that only those who have lived through it really understand.

It was general policy that when a GI recovered enough to be discharged he would be sent back to the front lines, and not necessarily to the same outfit he had been with. Just because you got shot up or had shrapnel wounds didn't mean you'd be going home. If you could still carry a weapon you were going back to the front. There were guys who had been wounded three or more times who had to return to the front.

I didn't think that was fair. I figured that if you were wounded bad enough to get to the hospital and lucky enough to have survived, the least they could do was find something in the rear for you to do. Not that anyone wanted it, but "a million dollar wound" was one where you lost a leg or an arm or were shot up bad enough that you couldn't fight any more. We knew some of those guys.

[68]

Once in a while, when things were quiet, we'd talk about the possibility of being seriously wounded, and how we'd feel about it. Maybe this was some sort of group therapy, a term we never heard of in those days, that helped us face what might come. Most of us thought we could live with losing a leg (we'd hate to lose them both, though). We agreed that for the right-handed, losing our left wouldn't be all that tragic, and vice-versa, I suppose. Being blinded, for all of us, was the worst thing we felt could happen.

One of the things I was glad for was the fact that I didn't have a wife or even a steady girlfriend at home to worry about. I had never even thought about it until one of my married buddies got a "Dear John" letter from home. He was 21 years old and had been married only six months before he was drafted. His wife wrote him a letter saying that she missed him, but she had found someone else; she hoped he wouldn't be mad at her. He took it hard, and I felt sorry for him. There were a few others who got Dear John letters, but they seemed to take it in stride, or else they covered their feelings well.

When I returned to Cambridge after the war, I remember a GI who came home after being overseas for two years to find out that his wife had a six-month-old baby. Apparently, he never said a word about it and he and his wife continued on as though it was his. He confided to me that he couldn't expect her not to go out once in a while, not knowing if he would ever come home. Everybody in the neighborhood respected his decision and they stayed a happily married couple for as long as I knew them.

Personally, it didn't bother me to see dead Germans after a battle but seeing a dead GI really got to me. Some of them had missing body parts from shells exploding near them. One day in Nuremberg, after a couple of days of heavy fighting, I saw the body of a dead GI who had part of his skull blown away, exposing his brain. As I walked past, a sigh came from his mouth. I almost jumped out of my skin. I knew he couldn't possibly be alive, but he had to have been killed just a short time before I got there. I don't know who he was but it was something I've never forgotten.

Next to these memories are some good ones. I remember well, for example, our first shower after being on the front line for a couple of months. My unit was going to a rear echelon area to take it easy for a few days. The Army had set up large open-end tents with shower facilities that accommodated ten or twelve guys at a time. Well, we were in a small German town and the tents had been set up in the middle of a park, in view of any German citizen passing by. Some of the Frauleins hooted and hollered at us and some of the guys waved back at them with whatever they were holding in their hand at the time.

We were allowed 15 minutes each to shower. It was sheer bliss to stand under that hot water and get soaped up and clean again. I think most of us had to be prodded out of the tents. We were given clean clothes, which was another big treat. You'd think we'd stink to high heaven after sleeping in our clothes for a couple of months, but I believe the cold weather helped.

Once dried and dressed, we were sent up the street for a "short-arm inspection." For the uninitiated, a short-arm inspection is a check for venereal disease. You have to take out your penis and "milk" it down so the medic can see if there is any sort of discharge, an indication of a venereal disease. We didn't know we were in for that, and we certainly hadn't anticipated standing in the middle of the street in front of rows of apartment buildings with civilians walking along the sidewalks.

We were in platoon formation as we marched up the street. Our lieutenant called, "platoon halt, right face, at ease, and get 'em out." I guess we hesitated a few seconds too long because he yelled: "I said get 'em out." I don't know when the first signs of the disease show up if you have contracted VD, but these guys hadn't been near a girl in several months or more. I was glad I was in the third row back. Some of the guys were, understandably, self-conscious—after all, people were all around us, ogling and obviously amused—and some, I guess, said to themselves. "Oh,

[71]

what the hell" and whipped them out. As you might have expected, nobody had any indications of VD.

No sooner was that over, when the word came down that we were going back to the front lines. Our replacements were under heavy attack and needed reinforcements. Needless to say, that news didn't set too well with us. One joker got a laugh when he said, "Look at it this way, guys. If you get hit or killed, at least you'll have clean shorts." Fortunately, the attack didn't last long and we all made it back. What made a lot of guys bitch was the fact that we had to hike the seven miles back to where we had just come from.

When we got back we found out that we were going to get a few days' rest in a small French farming community. We were to stay in a big barn, up in the hayloft. There was a rickety ladder we climbed each night to bunk down in our new "hotel." On my very first night, I started up the ladder to the hayloft and when I was on the top rung, reaching for the loft with my right foot, the rung broke. I fell about 10 feet and landed on my back. I had the wind knocked out of me but I seemed to be okay at the time. The next morning, though, my right leg had swollen, as it had when I hurt it in basic training.

The lieutenant wanted me to go to the field hospital but I asked him to let me rest for the day. He agreed with the warning that if it wasn't better the next day, I'd have to report to the hospital. I didn't think about taking advantage of that situation. I wanted to stay with the guys I knew. Thankfully, it did clear up enough that I could get around on it.

Being from the city, I didn't know that a lot of barns have very large rats that run around at night, seemingly not at all bothered by our presence. They'd run over us at night while foraging for food or whatever their mission is for the night. I used to tuck my feet and my head inside my blankets to keep them from getting next to me. After a couple of days, I more or less got used to it. Harder to adjust to was the smell of the manure that the farmers piled up outside of the barns.

The streets were really dirt roads muddied with cow urine and rain. We had to cross the road in front of the barn to get to the chow area. We would pull up our trouser legs to keep from splashing on them and put our mess kits inside of our jackets to keep them clean. Then, very gingerly, we'd make our way across.

The first morning there, we all headed for breakfast around 7:00 A.M. I was surprised to see a little boy, probably about 5 or 6 years old, herding cows down that sloppy road. I think he was barefoot. He was behind the last cow, waving a stick in his hand and shouting for them to move along. He was just about as tall as the cow's rear end.

The instruction and the tasks continued. The one I found I enjoyed the most was learning to use explosives. We made hand grenades from ¼ pound blocks of TNT. We'd attach primer cord to trees to blow them down across roads to create roadblocks, and we learned how to make a string of bombs. All this, of course, was done about a mile away from the village.

On the last day of these exercises, we still had about half a case of quarter-pound dynamite sticks. Our lieutenant decided we'd blow the whole thing at once just for the hell of it. We selected a spot just below the crest of a hill that we had been using for the explosives course and dug a hole about two feet deep in which we put the box of dynamite. We used a fuse long enough to give us plenty of time to get to a safe distance.

We lit the fuse and ran to a spot about 100 yards from the dynamite. Suddenly, to our horror, a woman, leading two horses pulling a wagon, was approaching from the other side of the hill. No one had seen her when we planted the explosive and for a while it seemed that nobody was ever going to see her or the horses again. We all started yelling to get her attention, but she either didn't see us or couldn't hear us.

She was about 50 yards from the dynamite when it exploded with a tremendous noise, throwing dirt and rocks into the air. The horses reared up, throwing her to the ground, and then ran off. We raced to the woman's side expecting the worst. Much to our amazement, she was only shaken up—actually, she was scared out of her wits. She got to her feet and, after surveying what had happened, let loose a tirade of French that we probably didn't want translated. Needless to say, we were glad that we left the area the next morning. I have no idea of where we went from there. I only know that it was back to the front lines.

CHAPTER 7: FOUL-UPS, MISHAPS AND NARROW ESCAPES

After sleeping out all winter it was good to know that warmer weather was coming—and to get the word we would be moving out shortly. We still had to dig foxholes every night but just for one, just big enough to give a little protection from enemy shelling or sniping.

We were stationed for a few days in a little French town called Wimmenau. One of my buddies approached me one afternoon and asked if I'd like some boiled chicken. He told me he had found a chicken wandering around behind a barn so he took it (spelled s-t-o-l-e) with the idea of cooking it that night. This had to be a top secret undertaking because stealing from civilians was a serious offense. I just assumed this country boy knew what he was doing. He invited another one of our buddies and I had no doubt when the three of us met that night in the cellar of an old barn that this was going to be a fine evening.

It was pitch black in that cellar and all we had for light was the small fire he had built to cook the chicken over. He filled his steel helmet with water and tossed in the chicken, plucked, gutted and cut up.

For the fire we were using a few empty K-ration containers. With their waxed coating they burned very nicely. As it cooked, it sure smelled good.

After an hour or so, our buddy fished out a piece of chicken with his bayonet and tested it to see if it was done. He said it tasted pretty good so we all tried it. It was tender and actually quite flavorful. We ate the whole thing, put out the fire and headed back to the house where we were billeted. I was in the attic with several others and we all slept on the floor. About 2 o'clock that morning I woke up with a terrible stomachache that quickly let me know I was going to have to beat it to the outside latrine on the double.

I made it to the top step when it hit me full force: I left a trail from the attic all the way to the ground floor and into the latrine. My belly was so bloated I couldn't fasten my pants. I stayed outside the rest of the night. By morning I found out that my two chicken-eating buddies were suffering the same fate. It appears the chicken had not been fully cooked and we had eaten it raw.

And of course that wasn't all. The woman who owned the house contacted our commanding officer, demanding that the person or persons who had crapped all the way from the attic to the first floor, be made to clean it up. I think her husband reported a chicken missing. Our commanding officer did not need to ask who was responsible. We had guilt written all over us. He had a talk with us and decided we had been punished enough. He sent us to the first-aid station where we were given some paregoric. To our great relief, it went to work right away. In case you're wondering who cleaned up the mess, I don't know, but it wasn't me. I think it was well over a year before I could eat chicken again.

When the orders came down to move on out, we left as usual, having no idea where we were headed. Those decisions were not ours. Our job was to take whatever objectives we had been delegated to capture or occupy that day. On the way to one of these objectives we ran into a natural obstacle: a frozen canal. Since the ice was not thick enough to walk across, we thought we could take a little running start and jump. After all, it was only about eight feet wide. The first guy to jump took off his heavy coat, field jacket and helmet. He handed his rifle to the fellow who would be jumping next. There was a little bit of ground extending into the canal that shortened the distance to three or four good running steps. He made it without any problem. Then the next fellow threw him his gear and he did the same thing. I was the last one to make the jump, and I didn't fare as well. After I had thrown my rifle and gear across to one of the guys, I managed to land on the little piece of ground on the other side, but it had become weakened from all the jumps before me and so it broke off when I hit. I went through the ice into the canal.

I was immediately pulled out but I was soaked through. There were no dry clothes to put on and my platoon had to keep moving on. I was told to get back to headquarters as soon as possible. I found a foot bridge about 100 yards up from where we had crossed. Then I had to hike about half a mile to the building housing our headquarters.

By the time I got there I was shaking uncontrollably. I was taken over to the fireplace where a good fire was going and immediately stripped down. Someone brought me towels and helped rub me down, and someone got me some hot coffee. Finally, the shakes quit and I started to feel human again. My clothes had been dried by the fire and were toasty and ready to put on again. As I dressed, I was thinking that I'd be able to stay the night in the nice warm building—maybe on a real bed.

About that time an officer came by and asked me how I was doing. I told him I felt great. In that case, he said, report back to your outfit. I should have lied. The end result was my sleeping out in the cold and snow, again, with my buddies. Some officers just had no compassion for us poor front-line infantry boys.

In fact, that was one thing we all hated. As infantrymen, we took pride in our unit, and didn't take kindly to it when the rear echelon brass gave front-line duty to anyone who fouled up in the rear.

As a result we got some pretty sorry characters. However, it didn't take us long to give them an "attitude adjustment." All we had to do was make them first scout one day and second scout the next day. They duty of the first scout is to lead the squad by going out in front about 30 or 40 yards to see if he can draw any enemy fire. The second scout follows by a few yards and tries to ascertain where any fire may be coming from.

Our intent was to get the message across that they were going to have to rely on us if they wanted to survive and we had to be able to rely on them. This was the quickest and most efficient, albeit a very dangerous way to make these guys realize that we weren't playing games. I think they all got the message when they realized they could be killed at any time. One fellow sent up to the front with us had been a sergeant with the 8th Air Force in England. Whatever he had done must have been pretty serious to get shipped out of England. As I recall, he turned out to be a good soldier.

Like night patrol, serving as first and second scout was also rotational. I think I had a fatalistic view about my turns as first scout. Having learned that the German snipers were excellent marksmen, able to kill you with one shot to the head, I figured that if one got me, I would never know what hit me.

One time when I was first scout, a sniper decided to let me get closer so he could shoot and kill the second scout, who was about 20 yards to my rear, and then knock me off, an easy mark since I was even closer. When I heard the second scout get hit, I immediately hit the ground and rolled a few times. I think the sniper took off after the first shot, realizing his plan had failed. The second scout had been killed instantly. I guess it was by the grace of God that the sniper had decided that day to take out the second scout rather than the first.

I remember one obnoxious joker who had been sent up by the CO from the rear. He thought he didn't have to do anything he didn't want to. He never said a good word about anything or anybody. He was another pain in the ass like the corporal we had in basic training. However, that was going to change. On his first day with us, we made him first scout. After a few yards, he turned around and asked why we weren't coming. We told him that we were waiting for him to get shot so we'd know where the enemy was located. You should have seen the look on his face. He changed his ways fast! No more wise-ass attitude from that boy.

Two foul-ups that had been sent to us were *really* no good. In all our efforts to straighten them out, nothing seemed to work. Looking back, I'm surprised they didn't go AWOL. After a heavy firefight one day, they were found hiding in a barn. Our platoon sergeant decided they needed a real "talking to" and went in the barn after them. No one saw what happened, but the guys came out with bloody noses and body bruises. The sergeant managed to get them transferred out of our unit.

I know I wasn't getting a sound night's sleep, but I didn't really feel that tired most of the time. It did catch up with me one day, however. We were advancing to an area known to be occupied by Germans. I had crawled up an open patch of field to the crest of a small hill. I found bushes I could hide behind and still see through. Nothing was moving ahead of me. I hadn't heard any word from our sergeant to continue the advance.

Our sergeant, who was in command of our platoon of approximately 22 men at that time, got his orders from our platoon officer who in turn got his orders from the company commander. The commander was at times a few hundred yards behind us, but sometimes, when there was close fighting, he was with us almost side by side. We had a lot of casualties and our platoon officer didn't last long. Our sergeant, on the other hand, seemed to lead a charmed life. He always came through a firefight.

Anyway, I must have shut my eyes for a moment. I awoke with a start to see one of our tanks parked about three feet from me. Tanks make a lot of noise when they're on the move and you feel the ground shake. I hadn't heard it come up so I guess I was sleeping hard.

All that day I found myself wondering whether the tanker had seen me or not. He never came out of his tank or even opened the hatch, so I couldn't ask him. If he hadn't seen me, I could have been flattened. On the other hand, maybe he hadn't seen me and just missed me, or maybe he saw me and decided to just pull up to park for a while. Thinking about it later, I would hate to have been killed accidentally. Of course, I wouldn't have known it, so why worry?

On some overcast nights if we were suspecting a German counterattack or if we wanted to advance under cover of darkness we had the support of "artificial moonlight," actually, an Army unit to our rear. It reminded me of back home when a movie theater was showing a "blockbuster" and rigged up two or three huge searchlights to traverse the sky in search mode. Our army unit would shine their searchlights on the clouds in a similar way, except the lights were not moving about. The reflection would give us just enough light to let us detect any movement in front of our position. Although the Germans could see us as well, we were more intent on finding open fields that may have been mined. The night my platoon went through the minefield, I'm sure we hadn't called for any artificial moonlight.

[83]

While we were going through the forests of the Vosges mountains, I couldn't see more than about 50 yards ahead of me. All I could see was perhaps 10 or 15 buddies working their way through. The day we got through the forest, we came to the open expanse of clear land. It's only a guess but I'd say it was open for at least a mile to my left and right and probably one half mile to a big hill in front of me. As I looked to my right, my platoon and several others were exiting the woods about the same time. I hadn't seen that many GIs, probably only 40 or 50, in a long time. With that many, I thought, there was no way the Germans were going to win.

We advanced across the field, toward the hill, which was on the outskirts of a town we were going to capture. Suddenly we saw someone riding a bicycle along the road that headed into town. We immediately opened fire on him, but not a single shot hit him. He hadn't seen us until we started shooting. When he realized what was happening, he stopped the bike, got off, raised his hands over his head and yelled, "Kamerad, schiessen nicht," (don't shoot). He was an old man who had been to see a friend and was returning home. We told him to stay where he was and not to try to warn anybody. I think he was so scared, he couldn't move a muscle.

Nobody was shooting at us as we started up the hill: a good sign, I thought. Where all the civilians were at this time, I don't know. At least they stayed out of our way. As I reached the crest of the hill, I could see over several houses. At that instant, I heard machine gun fire and right in front of me I could see dust being kicked up from where the bullets were hitting. The trail was leading directly to me. Army training had made it almost a reflex: in a fraction of a second, I dropped and rolled to my right to avoid getting hit. It turned out be to a lone German soldier manning the gun from a church steeple. He was captured and that was that.

The Germans at this stage of the game were retreating at a fast pace, but one or two would be left behind to pick off any foot soldier they could. For them, it was almost a certainty they would be killed.

One event I remember vividly. We had reached the shore of the Danube. We were going to cross in small boats at a very narrow point of the river. We could see across on the other side of the river about 20 German soldiers waiting to surrender to us. As one of our boats got about halfway across, it capsized. What happened then was amazing. Three or four of the German soldiers took off their heavy coats and boots and jumped in to grab the GIs flailing about in the water, clearly unable to swim. They did get them out safely and they certainly scored a lot of points that day. You can't shoot somebody who just saved your life.

I think it was the Saar River we were crossing another time when we had a scary incident, even though looking back on it we laughed. There were about 20 of us in a large landing ship tank (LST) built to carry troops and supplies. There were a few more making the river crossing at the time. Further down the river, a huge debris fire was burning next to a bombed-out bridge. Our boat master got us going across the river when suddenly the engine quit. He tried to get it going again but didn't seem to be having much luck. The boat was drifting right toward the fire and we certainly could not jump in the river with all our gear on.

We were all starting to panic—we sure didn't want to die under those circumstances. A couple of GIs pointed their rifles at the boat master and told him he'd die before we would if he didn't get the $*#!*$#* engine started! On the next try the engine sprang to life and we got across in record time. Like I say, it's only when you survive that these stories are funny.

One cold night we were camped near a river, and from the other shore we heard German soldiers singing a song. It was so pretty that we joined in singing it with them. We didn't know the words but with the help of Al Stucki, who was fluent in German, we were soon able to sing it in German. The name of the song was "Lili Marlene." The famous singer Hildegarde made it one of the most popular war songs ever. (She died in 2005 at the age of 99). That was another incident that enabled us to forget that we were enemies, even if it was for just one evening.

At that time, we weren't getting shot at every day; in fact, some days we had it pretty easy and would sit around shooting the breeze. One day we were guarding a German POW camp and one of the truck drivers who was going to transport them to another camp told us about these trips. Apparently, he had to have a certain number of prisoners standing up in the back, and some of them would give him a hard time when a few would pile on and there was no room for any more. Smirking, he told us how he solved the problem. When they griped, he'd say OK, and then close up the tailgate and drive toward the end of the camp. Then he'd turn his truck around, step on the accelerator, get up to about 60 miles an hour and slam on his brakes. Now there's room for more, he'd say.

No sooner had he finished the story when we heard a gunshot coming from inside the compound. Actually, most of us weren't surprised, knowing that no matter how many times the prisoners were searched, there were always a few guns hidden very well. The truck driver asked us what that noise was and we told him it was probably a gunshot. Then we suggested that since he was a big, exceptionally strong fellow, we'd let him go in and check it out. He got wide-eyed and said, "Not me. You the combat boys, I'm just a truck driver," and with that he ran back to his truck.

CHAPTER 8: FIGHTING VILLAGE TO VILLAGE

After guarding the POWs for a day, we were once again on the move. We arrived at a small village that had farms of varying sizes. Besides individual farmhouses, some areas had what I call row-houses. Like present-day condos, the buildings were joined together. Each unit had a cellar, a first-floor living area and bedrooms upstairs. We knew we were going to have to search every house, room by room looking for any German soldiers that might be hiding there. So, even though it looked peaceful and quiet, we could be in for trouble.

I don't know how it happened, but all the civilians in the village got the word that we would be searching every house for German soldiers. They were told to leave the doors to every room open so that we could easily see into them. Even doors to closets were to be open.

German soldiers has spread the word that the GIs in our division were going to rape the women and girls and kill all civilians. The civilians referred to us as the Amerikanisch SS." The German SS had a reputation for brutality that struck fear into German citizens, and so, their believing we were like them made things tougher for us. For one thing, they left the doors closed and you never knew if there was someone on the other side of a door waiting to kill you as you opened it.

I remember one time two of us were on the second floor of a house and all the doors along the hallway were closed. Everything was fine until we got to the last door. It suddenly opened and a hand grenade came flying out at us. The door was immediately slammed shut. My buddy picked up the grenade almost the second it hit the floor and opened the door and threw it back into the room. We hit the floor about the same time the grenade exploded, blowing part of the door off. I'm sure his split-second response saved our lives. It was a brave thing to do, but self-preservation is a powerful motivator. Neither of us bothered to look in the room to see whether anyone in there was dead or alive.

Meanwhile a small group of German soldiers had set up machine guns and an 88-millimeter artillery weapon about a half mile outside of town. (Although the 88 was basically an anti-aircraft weapon it was also used as an anti-personnel weapon—and it was deadly). Whenever they saw a GI emerge from a building after a search, they would open fire. Just before we took our last step onto the sidewalk, we'd take a deep breath and run like hell for the next doorway.

Sometimes, in the midst of it all, the tension is relieved by some crazy incident you don't expect. We were, again, searching the houses, room by room, for German soldiers. My squad was on one side of the street and Frank's squad was searching on the other side of the street. I was headed for the next doorway myself when I spotted Frank coming out of the building across the street. Evidently he had found a tall silk hat in one of the houses and had put it on. As if that weren't enough, he was pushing a baby carriage with his helmet and rifle in it. Casually strolling toward the next doorway, he tipped his hat to us and said, "Good morning, gentlemen."

Just then a couple of bullets hit the baby carriage. Frank grabbed his rifle and helmet and said, "Enough of that shit!" and bolted for the next doorway. I'm glad to say that Frank survived the war and he and I correspond to this day. We might have called him a "crazy bastard," but he gave us a good laugh and something to remember.

We finally got to the last house in the row on my side of the street. It was occupied by a man, his wife and young daughter. The man, who was probably in his mid-forties, had a long beard and a handlebar moustache that made him look older. Why he was home we never found out and didn't really care. He may have been a soldier at one time, gotten wounded and sent home.

It seems that when the Germans were firing their 88 at us, they hit a large barn in a field in back of their house, and it was ablaze. We saw the woman and her daughter carrying water back and forth in a valiant attempt to put out the fire. Their "fire brigade" was hopeless. For one thing, the containers they were using to hold water looked like large wall vases that had straps on them. They probably held a couple of gallons of water. The women slung them over their heads and, when they reached the fire, they would extricate themselves from the strap and throw the water on the fire.

When the mother saw us, she started screaming and yelling. Al, given his fluent German (his family had got out of Germany very early in the war) told us that she was blaming us for the fire that was making short work of her barn. Because this area had been in the middle of the action for some time, he asked her if she knew what American guns sounded like. (There is a difference in the sound of American and German guns.) She said yes. He asked her if she knew what German guns sounded like. Again she said yes. He asked her if she had heard any American guns that morning. She thought about that for a while and then answered no. He told her that the American artillery knew we were there and they were certainly not going to be firing on their own. Then he explained that it was the German 88 up the road that had unleashed the firepower that set her barn on fire.

Once she found out that we were not to blame for her loss (the barn was totaled) this woman, who had worked on a farm all her life we learned, and was a "strong as any man," went into her basement and brought out a keg of beer. Most German citizens, I believe, were good, decent people who, like us, were caught up in a war they really didn't want.

Meanwhile, however, her husband was sitting on a bench near the back door glowering at us. You could tell that he was getting madder by the minute. His daughter was giving the enemy his beer and he didn't like it. He held his tongue and kept quiet until one of the guys in the squad who carried a B.A.R. (Browning Automatic Rifle—a large weapon) pointed the rifle at the guy's head and said in broken German, "Amerikanish Soldaten Gut, Ja?" which hopefully meant, "American soldiers are good, right?" The old man began to tremble and all he could say was, "Ja, Ja, Gut Soldaten." We invited him to have a beer with us, but he declined.

While we were having our glasses filled another GI platoon had circled the Germans with the 88s and captured them. We moved to the front of the house and sat on a patch of lawn to watch the prisoners being marched by, their hands folded on top of their heads. The look on their faces as they saw us enjoying a leisurely beer, and then having to hear her chew them out for setting her barn on fire, was one of those moments you don't forget.

Frank and the baby carriage incident reminds me of something he wrote to me years later. Answering one of my letters, he said, "I had to laugh when you mentioned the smell of turds in a foxhole. Man, didn't they stink." I hadn't thought about that incident in a long time. It happened when Phil and I had reached the crest of a big hill that overlooked the valley leading up to the dug-in Germans at the Siegfried Line. We had made our foxhole in the early morning darkness and were about finished when daylight broke. It was deep enough so that the tops of our heads were just below ground level, but only wide enough for us to sit facing each other, toe to toe.

A few minutes into daylight I noticed some dirt being kicked up about a foot to the left of Phil's head. Since we had dug it on a hill, it was slanted a little bit and he was slightly higher than I was. I told him he better try to dig down another few inches because some sniper had him in his sights. Phil had been with us only a few days and didn't know yet that when you hear a loud bee buzz past your ear, it's not a bee. The bullet just missed him.

Soon after that I got the call from Mother Nature. Knowing that some sniper was waiting for us to give him something to shoot at, I wasn't about to get out of that hole. So, I got out my trusty shovel again and dug another hole beneath me as best I could. I managed to get my drawers down and complete my job without messing on myself. I covered it up but boy it did smell! I thought poor Phil was going to get sick.

About 20 or 30 minutes later, our platoon leader jumped into our hole, scaring the daylights out of us. Needless to say, it was now a tighter fit than it had already been. He was there to tell us that we were going to be getting out of there and when we heard his signal, three shots fired rapidly, we were to move out. I thought that was pretty good news until he told us that we'd be heading down the mountainside to cross the valley and try to get past the gun installations on the Siegfried line. I felt sorry for this guy because he had to locate all his men and that meant jumping in and out of tight foxholes, exposing himself to enemy fire. About ten minutes later we got the signal to move out.

At first we were running as fast as we could, zigzagging this way and that because we were getting shot at. However, because of the distance across the valley, maybe 3,000 feet, we tired in a short time. I didn't see anyone get hit as we crossed the valley, and I slowed down to a walk, still in a zigzag pattern. Lefty, who was in great physical shape, had run all the way across that open expanse and was halfway up the big hill, calling to the rest of us to hurry it up.

Suddenly we drew fire from an unseen gun position, and I saw Lefty hit the ground. I hit the ground in the same instant. Just as I looked up to see where he was crawling to, he got hit in the head by a bullet. He died instantly. A split second later, I got hit in the back of the head by a bullet. I was knocked out for several minutes and when I came to, I felt that if I checked the back of my head I was going to find a hole big enough to put my fist in. I was scared, and it was a minute or more before I dared to put my fingers to the back of my head. To my huge relief, I could tell it had just grazed my head and I wasn't bleeding all that bad. I figured I'd try to get the medic to bandage it up, but first I needed to retrieve my rifle and helmet. The force of that shot had knocked me a few feet away from my gear.

I started to move and got shot at again. The dirt was kicked up about a foot from my head so I knew a German had me, and anyone else near me, in his sights. I played dead until dark and then felt safe in getting my gear and heading back down the hill to a trench we had crossed coming up. I scared the hell out of a couple of GIs who had taken refuge in the trench, apparently to avoid the same gunner that got me. They told me they thought I'd been killed along with Lefty.

A medic was assigned to each platoon, as I recall, and he just happened to be in the trench I dove into coming off the hill. I got him to bandage my head, and managed to get a pretty quiet night's sleep in that trench. The next morning, things seemed to be under control and we were soon on to our next objective—

whatever that was; we never knew. The war, at that point at least, was one long "are we there yet?"

I don't know how long it took us to get used to being shot at, but we did. It wasn't long after this incident when the now familiar buzz zinged past *my* ears. My buddy said, "Somebody's got his eye on us but apparently he's a lousy shot." "Seems to me," I said," that he'd aim lower and go for a body shot." Well, it seemed the Germans would rather just wound us; that way it would take a couple of GIs to pull us to comparative safety and they would have fewer men shooting at them.

All of this we talked about as if we were having a discussion on war strategies and tactics in the comfort of someone's home, while the reality was that we were in the middle of nowhere in a foreign country, always alert to the possibility of being wounded or, worse, killed. Another irony that struck me that day was the fact that someone we don't know is trying to kill us on this beautiful warm, sunny day with white, fluffy clouds overhead. There was something almost ridiculous about the whole thing.

We survived in part by telling funny war stories when we had waiting time. One of my buddies had a helmet with a bullet hole over the right ear and an exit hole over the left, making it look like the bullet must have gone through his head. He would say that the bullet *did* go through his head but it missed all the

[97]

vital parts. Some said, "yeah, right," and laughed. What actually happened was almost as bizarre as his story. The helmet, when struck by the bullet, deflected upwards and the bullet passed out the other side. Then the helmet flopped back down on his head. He was a lucky GI with a damned good story for his grandkids.

My helmet was the mystery helmet. It had an exit hole but no entry hole. In answer to the questions I invariably got, I just said, "I don't know. I woke up one morning and there it was." In fact, I was on my stomach when I got hit and the bullet was fired at me from the rear, so the bullet grazed the back of my head and went out through the left side of my helmet. I was another lucky GI.

The next morning we started getting shelled with some "screaming meemies," rockets that "wailed" as they were fired through the air from a six-barreled rocket launcher. The term means a lot more than "jitters" to a GI who served in WWII. It was hard to determine how high up they were, but you could actually see them if you looked ahead of where the sound was coming from. We could hear them exploding to our rear.

I was leaning against the side of a small ditch when one landed about 100 feet away. After the explosion—it seemed like a long time to me, but it couldn't have been more than a second—I heard what sounded like a jeep coming up the dirt road I was on. I knew my senses were deceiving me: the sound was no jeep; it had to be a major hunk of shrapnel. It was decision time: do I stay hunkered down in the ditch or head for the gully on the other side of the road. The gully had been dug out by the Germans as a latrine. It appeared to be a little deeper and it might give me a little more protection, and even though it was probably full of you know what, I raced for the gully. As I hit the ground a piece of shrapnel hit the back of my neck and continued on. Sort of like skipping a flat rock on a quiet pond.

It didn't penetrate the skin, although, once again, it scared the hell out of me. I I hadn't chosen the gully for cover, which by the way, was partially frozen over, I might not have been hit at all. Then again, I may have been badly wounded or killed by a different piece of flying shrapnel if I had stayed in the ditch. After a few weeks of combat, you develop an attitude of "if it doesn't have your name on it, don't worry about it."

CHAPTER 9: SOMETIMES YOU SUCK IT UP

Still trudging mountainsides in German villages, one day we came across a German soldier lying on his side, his head resting on the downward side of the trail, his feet higher up. At first glance he sure appeared to be dead. He still had a pistol in his hand, and we eyed it as a nice souvenir for one of us.

As we stood there looking at the body, one of the guys said, "Does anything look funny to you fellas? Doesn't he have too much color for a dead man?" We had to agree, knowing now that once you're dead it doesn't take very long for the skin to turn gray. "I'd say he's pretending." At that, he pointed his rifle at the Germans's head and pulled the trigger. "Now, he doesn't have to pretend anymore," he said, as he picked up the Kraut's pistol. With that we continued on up the trail.

I think it was the next day that I saw something that has stayed with me all these years. We were going down a dirt road accompanied by a couple of tanks. We came across the body of a German soldier. He hadn't been dead too long because he still had some color in his face. The body was in the bend of the road and we just walked around it. The tank drivers, however, either didn't see the body or didn't care. They ran over it with their tank treads. After the two tanks has passed over the body, it looked like a flattened mannequin. Nobody said anything but I imagine I'm not the only one to remember that incident.

Over the next few days we had some rough encounters. Several GIs were killed and wounded. One of my buddies found himself out in the open and getting shot at. He managed to pull a couple of dead bodies around him for protection. I believe he had been assigned to carry a Bangalore torpedo to detonate under some barbed-wire fencing to give us a way through. Unfortunately, the thing exploded prematurely and he suffered a severe head wound. He was evacuated to the States and eventually recovered, although he had to have a metal plate put in his skull. I found out a couple of years ago that he had managed to live a happy life with his family and children before he died.

I hadn't realized how accustomed we had become to being shot at and shelled, until one day when my squad came across a small farmhouse in the path of our advance. An old man lived there by himself, and he took our presence rather matter-of-factly. We searched the house for anyone he might be hiding and also for any potatoes or bread we might be able to put our hands on. To our delight we did find about a dozen eggs the old man had put in the cellar.

To show him that we were good guys we gave him some of our K-rations to compensate for his loss of eggs. We went to the kitchen, found a frying pan, and opened a can of corned pork loaf. We fried that until we had a fair amount of grease in the pan and then added the eggs. Man, it smelled good.

Just about then, a shell exploded maybe 50 yards from the house. Apparently a German artillery spotter in the area had called our location back to his artillery unity. The old man told us we should take cover in the cellar. Our mouths watering for those fried eggs, we weren't about to let one shell keep us from our unexpected treat. Another shell hit in back of the house and the old man disappeared into the cellar.

We just shrugged our shoulders and continued to put our breakfast together. At that point, another shell exploded about ten feet from the kitchen door, blowing it off its hinges. We grabbed the frying pan with its precious payload, and joined the old man in the cellar. Lady Luck was with us: no more shells came in and we were able to enjoy our eggs.

And that wasn't the end of our good fortune: we were going to spend a night inside the farmhouse on a featherbed. This was my first time in at least three months to sleep in a house, let alone on a featherbed. The bed could hold three of us, even with our clothes on. We decided to draw straws to see who would get to sleep in the bed. I was one of the lucky ones. At least I thought I was. I tossed and turned for an hour before I finally got up and let someone else have my space. Oddly enough, I was more comfortable on the floor. The next day, however, I woke up with a head cold. Ironically, I had slept out all winter in a snow-covered foxhole and when I finally get a chance to be inside a house I catch a cold.

We continued to have encounters with German soldiers along the way and to lose men. It was rather strange to many of us that the same few GIs managed to survive. When the fighting finally ended, another fellow and I were the only ones left out of the group I had joined in January. Some survivors of various tragedies reportedly ask "why them and not me?" I have to say that thought never occurred to me. I felt sorry for any GI that was killed or severely wounded, but I was just grateful that I had survived.

Sometime later that day we saw the platoon on our left flank being held up by a small group of Germans manning a machine gun. My squad had come up behind a couple of empty houses and we could see the action going on about 500 yards to our left.

Our guys couldn't advance, however, because of the heavy fire being shot their way. From out of nowhere, one of our tanks came up beside me. I don't know if it was the same tank that almost ran over me but I sure was glad to see him. He opened the turret, stuck his head out and asked if he could help. I had him pull up past the building, pointed to the area where the Germans were, and told him it would help if he could fire into that area. He got back in the tank, swung the gun around and cut loose with a couple of well-placed rounds. I'm sure our guys were happily surprised.

As I watched, I could see a German soldier running toward the town. He wasn't much of a target at 500 yards but I felt I had to at least shoot in his direction. I took aim, gave him a little "Kentucky windage," (estimating where he'd be by the time my bullet got there) and fired. I couldn't believe my eyes when I saw him fall. Either he had tripped at the same moment, got hit by someone else, or I had made the best shot of my Army life. One doesn't think, "Hey, I'm going to kill somebody." You just know it is one less soldier to worry about killing you. I'm sure they felt the same way toward us.

It started raining that afternoon as we moved into the small town. We received word that we were to stay put until further notice. As I sat on that muddy hillside getting soaked to the skin, I was overcome by feelings I hadn't experienced before. It may have been exhaustion, frustration at the way things were going, knowing that I'd be sleeping in wet clothes for a few days, or just the insanity of it all. I think that was the worst I had felt throughout my two years, in spite of other days that had been much worse as far as the fighting went.

CHAPTER 10: THE WORST WAS YET TO COME

Every combat man, although he may not show it, has some fear in his gut when he knows he's going into a dangerous situation. For me, I would get a knot in the pit of my stomach that reminded me of the feeling I got as a little kid when I had to go to the dentist all by myself. But once you are in the middle of the fighting and the bullets are whizzing all around and you are firing away yourself, you forget the fear. You're too busy doing what you're there to do.

After my first few days of actually getting swept up in a shooting match with the enemy, getting shelled and seeing the wounded and dead all around me, I got to the point where I wasn't bothered by the carnage I saw. A numbness settled in and it stayed with me for a long time.

Nuremberg was the toughest fighting I had yet encountered. The city was in ruins except for a few apartment houses on the outskirts. Streets were filled with rubble, which made it very difficult to make any headway. That, plus the fact that we were being shot at every time we showed ourselves, made for a harrowing time. Our main objective, once we got to the hotel that was going to be our jumping-off point, was to get across the street and either kill or capture the Germans who were firing at us from the cellars of the buildings on the opposite side of the street.

We holed up in the bombed-out ruins of what had been a fine hotel. We could see sky when we looked up. I think it may have been an eight-story structure before it was hit. We took cover on the first floor where we could see across the street to where the Germans had been firing at us. In the basement was a wine cellar with maybe a hundred unbroken bottles of wine as well as bottles of Scotch, whiskey and bourbon. A lot of my buddies were very tempted to open a bottle or two but, much to their credit, I didn't see anyone do it.

The booze didn't tempt me, but a beautiful rifle I came across in the cellar of the hotel did. It was an "over and under"; that is, two barrels, one above the other. The top barrel used .22 caliber bullets, the bottom used .410 shotgun shells. The stock was beautifully engraved and it must have been somebody's pride and joy at one time.

I decided that I wanted to appropriate it, but first I'd need to find a hiding place until I could get back to it. I remembered one room on the first floor that was wall-to-wall rubble. The door to the room was open. It seemed like a good hiding place. I managed to pull the door far enough away from the wall to ease

[107]

the rifle behind it. My thinking was that if the fighting died down some I'd come back and get it.

Meanwhile, we had a lot of "cleanup" to do, and my trophy would have to wait. Our squad leader, Carl, was a guy we all had great respect for. For one thing, he wouldn't ask you to do something he wouldn't do himself. Squad leaders generally get volunteers or just tag some soldier to do a particular job. At that time, he needed to get a man on the other side of the street to get a foothold in one of the buildings and maybe give the Germans some trouble. Carl said he'd try to get across the street and, while we were trying to get him to let one of us go, our assistant squad leader, Charlie, took off zigzagging across the street.

We immediately started firing at the basement windows to make it difficult for them to get a shot at him. I can still see him falling as he got hit. Carl immediately tried to get across the street to help him, and he, too, was hit. I think he died instantly but Charlie was still alive. He had been shot in the stomach and was in obvious pain.

It's very hard for me to describe the situation. Here was our buddy, severely wounded, calling for help, calling for his mother, and we couldn't get to him. When our medic tried to get to him, the Germans shot at the medic, also. Our buddy died about 20 minutes later. It was a bad day for me emotionally.

Seeing two guys I really liked and had respect for get killed before my eyes really got to me. The two of them had been talking about buying a farm together when they got back home to Kentucky. The thing that was so sad was that the war ended a week later for all practical purposes. Although we didn't know it at the time, Nuremberg was our last battle.

Shooting at a medic is a violation of the Geneva Convention, which forbids shooting at an unarmed medic trying to help a fallen comrade. Incensed, we decided to rush across the street as a group, hoping that instead of getting picked off one by one some of us would make it. We took a deep breath and headed for a building that seemed free of any German activity.

Fortunately, we all got across safely except for one kid who got about halfway before he got shot in the foot. Somebody ran to pick him up and managed to carry him to the relative safety of the piled-high rubble. The kid was bleeding pretty bad. At this point, the soldier who had carried him to safety decided he'd have to carry him back to where we had just come from since he would be able to get medical treatment there. He felt it would be a safer trip this time because the Germans knew we were getting closer and they'd be taking off themselves. (I saw the guy a few weeks later and was glad to see he was okay.)

Now that we were across the street, the job was to get the Germans who were still firing at us from the end of an alley that ran behind the row of stores. The alley, which was probably only 150 feet long, was also littered with debris, which gave us some cover but made it difficult to scramble over without exposing ourselves. Every time we moved, the Germans fired at us from their machine guns.

We decided the only way to advance up the alley toward the Germans' position was to do it in short sprints—about 30 feet—jumping into cellar holes for momentary cover. I volunteered to cover the guys from behind piles of rubble while they were lined up to make a dash for it at my signal. When I yelled "Go!" the first man in line was to run as fast as he could and dive into that cellar hole. As soon as he took off, I would start firing at the machine gunners. It worked pretty well up to the last guy in line. I told him that when I yelled to he'd better be moving because I'd be right behind him running for my life, too. This kid had been with us only a few days and this might have been his worst experience to date. I yelled, GO! fired a few rounds, and started running. I beat the kid to the hole. He made it, but I told him he was going to have to learn to run faster if he wanted to stay alive.

Our plan was to try to zigzag up the alley by crossing it and getting into one of the stores across the way. It was a shorter distance running across the alley than it was trying to find an open place on the same side. Two of us made a break for it and got into the store when it suddenly dawned on us that this was the building the shots came from that killed Charlie and Carl. We knew that if only a couple of Germans were still there, they were going to be very quiet. We found a trapdoor and, standing to one side, very cautiously opened it up. It was a suspenseful moment.

Our adrenaline was running high. We knew that anyone opening that door could be shot instantly. When no shots came from below we relaxed a little, but you never let your guard down. We yelled for them to come out. No response. My buddy eased down the steps and said it was too dark to see anything. "Well," he said, "I'll do this the easy way." He pulled out a hand grenade, told me to get out of the way, and then pulled the pin. He threw the grenade toward the end of the cellar and then flew up the steps and slammed the trapdoor shut. We dove for cover in a corner of the room as the grenade exploded. If the Germans were still there they wouldn't be bothering us anymore.

We still had to get to the machine gunners, who were still in a position to get us. Instead of trying to get back across the alley, we thought we could knock a hole in the wall between us and the next store. We used our rifle butts to knock a hole in the wall, which wasn't too thick, thank goodness. We felt pretty pleased with ourselves. We were ready to get right up to the Germans and take them by surprise.

About this time, we thought we heard a noise coming from the cellar of the room we had just left. "Maybe, the grenade didn't get them," I said. "Well, I can fix that," he answered. He walked over to the trapdoor, eased it open and threw in a phosphorous grenade, the kind used to start a fire and drive out anyone hiding in a building that we can't get into.

We couldn't hang around there, of course, and so we scrambled back to the store with the intention of breaking through another wall before the fire caught up with us. We were about to smash the wall when we felt it getting hot. It seems that some of our buddies, unbeknownst to us, had captured the German machine gunners and were now in the process of trying to flush out the ones who had killed Charlie and Carl. We had lost sight of each other and each group thought the other had gone ahead to another store. Like us, they decided that the best way to do what they had in mind was to use a phosphorous grenade.

My buddy and I were between a rock and a hard place: we had a brisk fire going on in back of us and now one in front. The whole time all this was going on, shells were exploding outside the building we were in, and we could hear machine guns—American and German—along with continuing small arms fire.

You're not aware of it when you are in the midst of it, focused on the job in front of you.

Sooner or later, we knew we had to get moving, so we located the back door, opened it, and looked across the alley. We thought we could get some cover there for the moment. We both took deep breaths and ran like hell. We didn't get shot at, which surprised us. It was then that we found out that our buddies had captured the machine gunners.

After the fighting was over in Nuremberg, we were holding two German soldiers who had surrendered. To have a German soldier give up was very unusual, so our interpreter asked them why they had. One of them said they had run out of ammunition and could no longer fight. Well, that was the wrong reason to give. It meant that otherwise they would still be trying to kill us. My buddy told me to take them out around the back of the building and shoot them. I hesitated and another GI stepped up and said he'd do it. He did, and that was the end of that. I didn't have any problem shooting a German while we were fighting but I couldn't just shoot one in cold blood. That was a part of me that I had been unaware of.

After those two days of real tough going, I was able to get back to the hotel, but, much to my unbelieving eyes, the rifle was gone. Someone must have seen me hiding it and decided they wanted it as much as I did. I think it had to be someone from a rear-echelon group. Anyway, I was fit to be tied but I couldn't do anything about it. It also bothered me to think that a guy in my own outfit would have taken it. Maybe there was another explanation. I'll never know.

Toward the end of what had been a long, long day, my buddy and I were coming out of another rubble-strewn alley when we spotted a photographer in an Army Jeep. Where the hell he had come from, I don't know but I guess he took his work seriously. He had to have been near the action all day. He said he was with *Life* magazine and wanted to take our picture. I don't think either one of us said a word; we just stared at him. We were exhausted and having our picture taken by some hot-shot photographer, even for a magazine as big as *Life* was the last thing on our minds.

He took a couple of quick shots of us and told us to look for the next edition of the magazine because we'd be in it. Even though I thought he was a wise-ass, I did write home about a week later and asked my mother to buy the magazine because I might be in it. My picture never did appear. My mother wouldn't have recognized me anyway. My hair was down to my shoulders and I had a beard. We probably looked like a couple of the GIs that Bill Mauldin drew and wrote about in his book, *Up Front*. We were a scraggly bunch.

CHAPTER 11: CLOSE TO THE END

We finally left Nuremberg and headed for Munich. We weren't looking forward to that at all. We felt that if the fighting in Nuremberg was bad, what would it be like in Munich, the headquarters of the Third Reich? I know I was dreading it.

Since the Germans were retreating so rapidly, we had to ride in trucks just to catch up with them. It was getting pretty close to the end of the war and I think we were nearing the Austrian Alps. I say this because it was snowing on us at the time. We had been on the trucks for about six hours or more that day and we were cold, hungry and tired. The motorized column came to a halt and we sat there for another two hours or so.

Finally, one GI decided he had enough and headed to a large building near the road to see if he could get some protection from the snow and cold. It didn't take long before we all followed him. He had broken a door down to gain entry and we piled in. Somebody decided to build a little fire in the corner of what turned out to be another warehouse. Before long we had a small blaze going and we were starting to get nice and warm.

I suppose we should have put someone in charge of the fire but we didn't. Pretty soon the whole corner was afire, enveloping pieces of furniture. We pulled ourselves together and headed back fast for the truck. By this time the night sky was beginning to glow from the flames. We had wondered earlier whether we were there to launch a surprise attack on the Germans, but now, if this was intended to be a secret mission, it wasn't going to be a secret for very long.

We stayed by the trucks all night. Most of the guys—and there were a bunch of us—were letting off a little frustration by hootin' and hollerin'. The officer in charge of the column had gotten drunk and couldn't be found; the officer sent to look for him never came back. In the aftermath of that fiasco, the top brass demoted several officers. Oh how we loved that!

I didn't know it at the time but a lot of my buddies were scrounging whatever they could in that warehouse. I found that out when the story got around about the German soldier we had taken. He had been a boot maker as a civilian and could make a pair in a day or two. I think his name was Fritz. One of my buddies had scooped up some sheets of leather he found. Why he had taken them, I don't know. Same reason I hid the rifle, I guess. It seems that for a carton of cigarettes this boot maker would make you a pair of boots. We saw one pair he had already made and they were beautiful. I put my name on the list to get a pair but as luck would have it, we were moved out before he had a chance to make mine.

I did get another German prisoner to sketch my profile. I still have it but I can't remember where or when it was done. Since it hadn't been folded, I assume it must have been done after I got back from overseas. A lot of German prisoners of war were sent to the United States to keep them from escaping back to their front lines. Some of them were located in the camp I was sent to upon reaching the States.

One of the most shocking things I recall from Munich was finding some SS troopers hanging in trees. They had been killed by the few remaining citizens who had managed to survive the war and they weren't about to let a few fanatics get them killed when the war was all but over. The people hung white sheets hanging from their apartment windows, signaling that they didn't want any more fighting—a big relief for all of us.

My platoon was put on guard duty around a German camp that held Russian prisoners, men and women, who had been forced to do heavy labor. The Russians were trying to escape and kill every German man, woman or child that they could and it was up to us to prevent that. We did see some Russian soldiers kill a couple of Germans by beating them to death. They were getting revenge for the atrocities the

Germans had committed against them in the beginning of the war.

I don't know who was responsible for getting them back to Russia but eventually they were all loaded on big trucks for the trip home. Of course a lot of them didn't have any homes or families to go back to so I have no idea of what became of them. While they were in camp, though, they were a handful. We had to have a guard about every thirty feet around the camp, night and day. Some of the DPs (Displaced Persons) had pistols and vodka, a bad combination, but no matter how many times we searched the camp we couldn't find a single pistol or bottle of vodka.

About two nights after I arrived at the camp one of the DPs got drunk and fired his pistol close to one of our guards. I think he was just fooling around but we didn't take it that way. Our CO said to overlook it this time and he'd have a talk with the prisoners, and he did the next day. That night, however, someone took a shot at us again. Although it was at least ten feet from the guard that had been shot at before, you never know when a bullet might ricochet and get you that way.

We complained to the CO and he said he had a plan. If we got shot at again, we were to hit the ground and each of us was to fire a few rounds into the camp. Well, that night, these playful Russian drunks were at it again. This time we all fired back into the camp. Luckily, no one was hit and that ended their fun.

On one of my day shifts, I saw a funny thing happen. There was a little stream running through a corner of the camp, and the Russian women would do their wash there. One day, a large woman was doing her wash, when a fist fight broke out between a couple of Russian guys. When she saw them, she walked over, grabbed each one by their shirt fronts and pulled them apart. Then what happened was like a scene from the patty cake routine Bob Hope and Bing Crosby did in the "Road" movies they made later. Both men looked at each other, nodded their heads and each swung a fist, one fight-handed and one left-handed, hitting the woman right in the face. She went down like a sack of cement and the two guys went right on fighting.

I don't know who sets up the schedule for guard duty but it was tough. We were on for three hours and off for six, 24 hours every day for two weeks. I didn't realize how exhausted I was until a week later, a buddy of mine, tweaked my nose hard enough to bring tears to my eyes. Once the tears started I couldn't stop. I must have cried for at least five minutes. He wanted to know what was wrong but I really had no idea. I think I was so tense all the time that when he triggered those tears my body just let it all go. I did feel a lot more relaxed after I finally stopped.

After guarding the DPs, five of us were assigned to guard a particular section of a reservoir to prevent anyone from poisoning the water. The perimeter was divided into sections and each group had its own area to patrol. Here it was three hours at a time and that gave us 12 hours to rest in between patrols—a lot better than the three on and six off we had just finished.

We were billeted with a German family in a small house near the reservoir. The owner was a German soldier who had lost a leg on the Russian front a couple of years before. His wife and two little girls stayed out of sight. We ate our rations and slept in what had been their living room.

With little else to do, we played poker a lot. The owner would come into our room at night, sit in a darkened corner and smoke his pipe while he watched us play. He never spoke a word to us and we didn't talk to him. I tried to imagine how I would feel if we had lost the war and some of the enemy had been billeted in my house. I know I'd be more than a little upset by it.

About the third night we were there, a 2nd Lieutenant came into the house to ask us about our schedule for patrolling the reservoir. We had been taught to jump to attention when an officer entered the room but given the circumstances of the war at that time, no one felt obliged to follow procedures.

The officer, probably one of those we called ninety-day wonders, seemed a little flustered when we just continued to deal the cards as we explained what our patrol schedule was. We even asked him if he'd like to play a couple of hands but he said he couldn't and then left.

Apparently, this little breach of protocol was not only unsettling to the officer, it was shocking to the owner. He got up out of his chair and hobbled over to us with his crutch under one arm and his pipe still in his mouth. When he reached the table he removed the pipe from his mouth and said in German, "Excuse me, please, but wasn't that an American officer?" We told him it was and with a look of disbelief, he told us, going through the motions as he did, that if we had been German soldiers and an officer came into the room, we would have immediately stopped whatever we were doing and come to attention. Had we not done that we would have been shot on the spot.

This man then went to another part of the house and brought his wife back with him. He told her what had happened and went through all the motions, again, of us dealing cards, an officer coming through the door, us just sitting there and continuing with our card game. He was so impressed by that act alone that he considered us guests at his house and not the victors of the war. We had become heroes in his eyes.

He had his wife do our laundry after that and he even brought his two little girls in to meet us.

A couple of days later some packages from home arrived and we eagerly opened them. I found a can of hard candies that I thought the little girls would like. When I offered them, their father said that if I didn't mind, he'd like to ration it out to them as they hadn't had any candy in years. I said that was fine and gave him the candy. The girls were about 4 and 6 years old and just as cute as could be. They each begged him for a piece and he was obviously glad to be able to give it to them. The look on their faces was priceless.

I couldn't help but think of the hard times that the families of soldiers, of any war, go through when their loved ones are wounded or killed. This family, like thousands of others, had to get by on whatever they could scrounge up. I thought of the folks at home complaining that they had no butter for their bread or no gas to put in their cars. They should see what the civilians in war-torn countries had to endure.

When it came time for us to leave, this family was genuinely sorry to see us go. We had become friends and that made us feel good. We shook hands with the owner and his wife and the little girls gave us hugs.

There was another incident that brought home to us how much starvation the civilians were going through. We were in a chow line one day when I noticed a little boy about five years old taking garbage out of the barrel where the GIs were throwing their uneaten food. He had a small pail and was filling it with whatever his little arm could reach. I got a couple of my buddies to come with me, including Al, of course. When we approached the kid, he seemed afraid—I suppose he thought that as enemy soldiers we might hurt him or something. Al asked the boy in German what he was going to do with the food. He said he was going to take it to his mother and sister. They were living in the cellar of a bombed-out apartment building. We told him not to be afraid and to go get his mother and sister and to tell them to bring something they could put food into.

While he was gone, we rounded up some more containers with the help of our cook and filled them with food. I don't remember exactly what we had, but I do remember creamed potatoes and English peas plus a few more items. We weren't too sure if the boy and his mother and sister would return but they did. The mother remained several yards away from us, so we brought the food to her. She cried as we handed her the containers of our dinner fare. She told Al that they hadn't had a warm meal in several days and that even that was only scraps. The little boy was stuffing the potatoes into his mouth with his bare hands. I think every one of us was feeling the heartbreak of the moment.

[124]

Scenes like that remain in my memory today. A lot of the horrors of war, dead bodies, bombed-out buildings, carnage everywhere, eventually faded, but the image of that starving boy and his mother's tear-filled eyes are one of those images that will live with me forever.

It was only a day or two later that we got word that the war was over and we would be heading home. I think I almost collapsed from that news. It was like a heavy weight had been lifted from my shoulders. It seemed like we all started talking again. I hadn't realized it before then, but over the past weeks we had all but stopped talking.

It turned out be to a good news/bad news day. Yes, we were going home for a 45-day furlough, but it was to rest up before they shipped us to Japan to help out in the Pacific war. It didn't go down well. I heard someone say, "Hey, we won our war, let them win theirs." Another said, "Once I get to the States, they will have to find me." I don't know how many would have tried to disappear, but, thankfully, the war in Japan ended about a month later.

CHAPTER 12: LOVE AND WAR IN PARIS

After pulling guard duty we were shipped to Camp St. Louis (San Lou-ee) in France. I believe we were about 100 miles north of Paris. We had been promised a week in Paris but that didn't happen. We slept in eight-man tents and ate in the mess hall three times a day. To keep us busy, they had us do close order drill for about an hour every morning and then police the area. Most of the day, however, we relaxed, read, played cards and chewed the fat.

A stage was set up at the camp, and a piano had been brought in for anyone who wanted to play. One fellow in particular could really play good Boogie-Woogie, which had become very popular. He had quite a repertoire—it seemed as if he could play just about anything we asked. The area became a very popular spot for most of us, and it sure helped pass the time.

I don't remember how it happened but I broke my glasses one day and was relieved from doing any little jobs the officers dreamed up to keep us occupied. Without my glasses, I couldn't read or even recognize anyone until they were 10 or 15 feet away, so I was pretty limited until my new glasses arrived about two weeks later.

I hadn't thought about it once while I was on the front lines, but what would have happened if I had broken them then? Would I be sent back to the rear or would I be expected to keep on going? It made me wonder. I had long ago acquired the nickname of "Cousin Weak-Eyes Yokum," a character from the popular Li'l Abner comic strip.

We did get daily trips into Paris as had been promised, but instead of the seven solid days we thought we had coming, we got only one day. The officer in charge of the camp decided to give everybody, from the front-line soldiers to the guys in all the support units, a taste of Paris. We were furious to begin with but most of concluded from celebrating that one day in Paris, boozing it up and getting next to some good-looking women, that we never would have survived seven days.

On the day of my trip to Paris I had to be on the truck by 4:00 A.M. The convoy of vehicles arrived in Paris about 8:00 A.M. Each truck held about 16 guys—that's crowded. If you've ever ridden in an Army "6-by" for four hours on hard wooden seats, you know what an ordeal it was, but I can tell you, the ride was worth it. We were eager to see everything and do everything.

The minute we got off the trucks in Paris, we were surrounded by three or four Frenchmen, all wanting to buy anything and everything we had. We

[127]

had heard that a carton of cigarettes was worth $20 American on the black-market. That was almost a month's pay. Since I didn't smoke, I had a carton and sold it right away to one of the buyers. They were asking us to literally take off our jackets, caps and boots and sell the items to them. Of course, we couldn't do that, but with what we did sell we had enough money to carry us through the day, sightseeing, drinking and dating a few lovely French girls.

One of the platoon officers with us said that the first place he wanted to go was the American Red Cross to meet some American girls. That sounded good to us. Some of us hadn't been near a girl in a year or more, and you can bet I was looking forward to this new adventure. We just knew the girls would fall all over us.

I have to admit that we did look pretty sharp in our new Eisenhower jackets. We wore all the medals we had earned in the campaigns we had fought plus ones for meritorious deeds; Bronze Stars, Silver Stars, Purple Hearts, etc. plus our new combat badges. (As graduates of Advanced Infantry Training we were given the rank of Private and qualified to wear the Infantryman's badge. The badge had a blue background with a silver rifle on it. After we got into combat we were promoted to Private First Class and given Combat Infantry badges with the silver wreath on it.) Yeah, we looked good.

We found out where the Red Cross Center was and the lieutenant led the way. As we entered the lobby a nurse looked at us and said, "Oh look here come Uncle Sam's paid killers." You could have heard a pin drop. The lieutenant walked up to her and said, "You bitch," and punched her in the face. She went down like a sack of potatoes. Then he turned to us and said, "Let's go fellas, this is no place for us." We were all in a state of shock about the incident. Who would have thought we'd hear that from an American nurse, and in a war most regarded—then and now—as righteous. I guess she never reported the incident because we didn't hear anything about it.

It didn't take long for us to get over it. We spent the rest of the day sightseeing, drinking and fighting off the French women. Well, not all of them. We had been warned by our officers that Paris probably had about 10,000 licensed prostitutes and 10,000 unlicensed, but they didn't know how many "amateurs" were operating. So yes, they were after us, but it was their way of making a living. Even so, it was still quite an experience for us to have beautiful women proposition us and make us feel special—it was unlikely to happen to most of us once back in the States.

Since prostitution was legal, the professionals were glad to show you their health certificates to assure you that they had no communicable diseases. Certificates were required by French law for those who wanted to be in the business. The Army provided us all with condoms. If you caught something you had better report it to a medic or face charges. They didn't want their soldiers in sick bay with a venereal disease.

The "houses" where these women plied their trade were magnificent. They had thick shag rugs, considered posh at that time, paintings on the walls, and lovely old furniture. Some of the girls offered mini stage shows along with their other services, and the show served as a drawing card to help you choose one place over another. After the show, the girls would line up and you'd take your pick. Wonderful! Still, I found it disconcerting to see a police station across the street from these houses. Even though prostitution was legal, it still made you wonder.

After each visit, the guys usually headed to a barroom for a cold beer. All the bars seemed to have "working girls" who would try to entice you into going upstairs with them. I suppose they were the unlicensed ones. So what started out as a famine and feast situation for us GIs turned into a feast and feast.

We had until 11:00 P.M. to make the most of the day. That's when the trucks would pick us up and return us to camp. If you weren't there on time the trucks left without you and you were considered to be AWOL. Some of the GIs had to be "poured" into the trucks; some needed a lot of help and others managed to show up sober. The ones who were drunk slept on the floor of the truck the whole way back—one way of avoiding the agony of a four-hour ride on hardwood seats in a crowded truck.

One of the camp rules was that everybody had to fall out for breakfast at 6:00 A.M. or face some kind of punishment. It was easy to tell who had been to Paris the previous day. They were bent over, still half asleep, some in the same clothes they had worn the day before, stumbling along the path to the mess hall. Finally, the camp commander took pity on the guys and the order came down that if you had been to Paris the previous day you didn't have to fall out for breakfast the next day. That improved morale by at least 1,000 percent.

One day we were doing some close order drill with a new 2nd lieutenant when we heard a lot of cheering going on about a quarter of a mile from us. The sound continued to get louder platoon by platoon until we finally made out the words: "The war's over, the war's over." Our lieutenant called the platoon to a halt, had us do a right face so we were facing him and had the gall to say, "Gentlemen, you've heard the news, you have 15 seconds in which to cheer."

That, my friends, went over like the proverbial lead balloon. We didn't say a word. We just stared at him. After about ten seconds of complete silence on our part, I think he realized he had made a big mistake. "OK fellas, you're all dismissed," he said.

[131]

We still didn't move or say a word. He abruptly turned around and walked off. About two seconds later, we all let loose. I think the biggest thing in our minds was not having to go to Japan.

The officer in charge of the camp called a meeting to tell us, officially, that the war had ended in Japan and we would be headed home in a few days. We were one bunch of happy GIs. We all started acting like a bunch of schoolboys, playing practical jokes on anybody we could. As I remember, everyone in the 45th Infantry Division was going to get a 45-day furlough. That's about all anyone talked about for the next few days.

I don't remember much from that day until I boarded the *Aquitania* that was to take us home. On the ship we busied ourselves playing crap games and recounting the close calls we had had—even things that were far from funny at the time but could be laughed at later.

We heard that there were some WACs and some nurses quartered up on the deck above the one we used during the day, and that many of them were available for $5 a turn. I did see a couple of long lines of GIs outside two of the cabins so I surmised that what we had heard was true. I was content to just shoot dice until my money ran out. Even though I did get seasick for a day, it was a nice trip home.

When we came into New York harbor, the captain, who was British, announced that in a short time the Statue of Liberty would be coming into view on our port side, so all the fellows on deck started for the left railing, hoping for a nice view. Believe it or not, the sudden shift of weight when some three thousand soldiers made their move actually caused the ship to tilt. The captain yelled through the sound system in his Cockney accent: "Now 'ear this, now 'ear this, we're coming in like a lame duck. Some of you chaps will have to go to the other side or we'll capsize." I don't think we were too upset by this warning but some of the guys did head for the other side yelling, "Some of you fat WACs, get over there!" That got a few laughs but I'm sure the WACs, if they heard it, didn't appreciate it.

I hadn't had a chance to see the Statue of Liberty when we shipped out for the front lines so I really wanted to see it this time. There was a lot of cheering once we got within sight of the statue. While looking at it, I couldn't help but think of the thousands of soldiers that would never see it. I considered myself a very lucky guy to have survived and gotten back in one piece.

An Army band was playing for us as we debarked from the ship. This time they were playing "Back in the Saddle Again." After landing and carrying all our belongings with us we boarded a train and headed for a processing center at a camp whose name I can't recall. I think it was in Maryland. I do remember that it was about 10:00 or 11:00 o'clock that night when we got our first meal. And what a meal it was! You could have just about anything you wanted. I remember having steak so tender you could cut it with a fork and a quart of cold milk to wash it all down. It's a meal I still remember.

The next day we started the processing that would get us new uniforms and the necessary papers for that 45-day furlough.

CHAPTER 13: FURLOUGH, FORT RILEY AND DISCHARGE

I arrived in Boston around the 1st of September, 1945 and took the subway to Cambridge. I called my folks to let them know I was on the way. How can anyone begin to describe the euphoria of being home again. All I can say is I was one happy fellow.

From Central Square in Cambridge, I took a streetcar to Putnam Avenue and walked the three blocks to where I lived on Kinnaird Street. As I walked down the hill, people on the street greeted me with "Welcome home, soldier," and that really made me feel good. By the time I reached my house, a lot of kids had gathered around me. I knew most of them and was surprised at how much they had grown.

When I walked in the front door to our apartment my mother had tears in her eyes. She threw her arms around me and said, "Thank God you're home safe." My stepfather shook my hand and said, "I'm glad you made it." My grandfather just shook my hand. I think he had a tear in his eye when I told them all how glad I was to be back with them.

The day I arrived home my mother cooked me a pan of cornbread and a pan of candied sweet potatoes.

I ate every bit of it. I spent the next few days getting used to being home. It was great just to sleep in my own bed again. So many little things that I used to take for granted looked different to me now—the street I lived on looked smaller, the kids I had known by name had grown up a lot and seemed like strangers, the guys I once played touch football with were no longer interested in that. One thing that put a smile on my face was the look on my *mother's* face when she discovered I was up before her and had made my bed. Not only that, but my clothes were hung up neatly in the closet, too.

After relaxing at home for a few days, I wanted to look up my buddies and find out how they had fared. I made a few calls first to make sure they were okay. I was quite relieved to find out that they had all made it through the war. We agreed to meet at a local pizza parlor, one of our old hangouts.

That evening I walked down the street and was again surprised at all the folks who greeted me with a "Welcome home, soldier." I found my friends, and we sat around eating pizza and reliving our days in the service. Two had been in the Navy and one had been assigned to submarine duty. He told us about some scary moments when his sub was depth-charged by the enemy. We still had time to serve before we'd be discharged, but that didn't bother us a bit. We had made it through the tough times.

That 45-day furlough just flew by. Before I knew it, it was mid-October and time to report back to Camp Swift, about 25 miles out of Austin, Texas. I had been transferred to the 2nd Infantry Division. Some of the guys in the unit I was assigned to had seen combat, so I was right at home. The ones I hung out with were a wild bunch. We'd go into Austin just about every night to have a few beers and dance with the girls at a honky-tonk place called the Iron Front Café. Just about anything and everything went on, it seemed, and it was all new to me. It's hard to realize now but I was only 19 years old at the time. There were girls on the make, GIs fighting, loud music playing—as we came to say later, "It was our kind of place."

It was here I learned about things that were never spoken of at home. An "old" woman—she was probably in her early 40s—hung out at the Iron Front, and one night she asked me to buy her a beer. I said sure. She thanked me and said, "I'd like to introduce you to my daughter, Nora. She's about your age and I know she'll show you a real good time." By this time I knew what that phrase meant so I said, "OK," not really knowing what I was in for. What struck me at the moment was that a mother would pimp for her daughter.

She called her daughter, who was sitting in a booth with another girl, to come over and meet me. She was rather good looking and wasn't at all shy. I asked her if she'd be interested in going out and she said she would. However, she added, she already had a date that night so we set it for the following Saturday night about 7:00 P.M.

The following Saturday night I got to the Iron Front around 6:30 and ordered a beer. When she still hadn't arrived at 8:00, I figured that she had stood me up. The girl she had been sitting with the night I met her came in about that time and told me that Nora had been picked up in San Antonio on charges of loitering and that she'd see me next Saturday. I thought that was better than getting stood up, so I thanked her, had another beer and went back to camp. The following week, Nora was at the bar. She never mentioned what had gone on in San Antonio. I really didn't care anyway. We had several good times over the next three months.

As Christmas time was rapidly approaching, all the GIs who hadn't had a leave in the past year were given two weeks furlough. I had started chumming around with one guy in particular as we seemed to hit it off. Since we had just gotten back in October from a 45-day furlough we couldn't talk the commanding officer into letting us go home for Christmas.

Those of us left in camp had to pull KP, barracks guard and maintenance duty for three days straight. KP wasn't too bad because there were so few GIs left in camp. Barracks guard was just a matter of being in the barracks for 24 hours to make sure nothing happened and maintenance duty meant keeping the fire stoked in the furnace for 24 hours. After our three-day stretch of duty someone else got the job and we were free to do whatever we wanted until our next three-day work stretch.

My buddy and I decided that if we couldn't get a pass to leave camp, and we were done with our three-day duty, why not just walk out the gate and go to San Antonio for the weekend. Who'd miss us? It wasn't a smart thing to do but we did it. We thumbed our way to San Antonio anticipating a great time. We got there on a Friday evening, started drinking, and the next thing I knew, it was Sunday morning and I didn't know where I was.

I was sitting in the middle of an empty lot and my nose was scratched up, my eyeglasses were broken and I had something I never had before—one helluva hangover. I was sick as a dog. I saw my buddy stretched out on a grassy spot about 20 feet from me and he seemed to be as bad off as I was except his nose was okay and he didn't have glasses to worry about.

He explained to me why my nose was scratched and my glasses were broken. The night before, after drinking all day, we were headed back to the YMCA where we had paid 50 cents for a bed for that night. He had to relieve himself and since I was too drunk to navigate on my own, he propped me up against a wall and told me to wait for him. He said he was just emerging from the alley when he saw me pass out and hit the sidewalk face first. He picked me up and was able to get me walking again. However, since he was just about as drunk as I was, he steered me to the vacant lot where we both ended up sleeping it off.

Well, I never went AWOL again; I never got that drunk again, and I think I learned a very valuable lesson about drinking. A few drinks may be okay but more is certainly not better. What scared me the most was not being able to remember anything of my weekend.

One Saturday afternoon, while I was still in Austin, I had an experience that shook me up. It brought home to me just how much I had been affected by the sights and sounds of the war. A couple of young boys, who were about 13 to 15 years old had sneaked up behind me while I was looking in a store window. They set off a couple of firecrackers and the second I heard the sound I flattened myself against the window. It was over in a couple of seconds. Even though I hadn't heard any gunfire in six months, my brain still took it as enemy fire. I turned on the kids and chewed them out for pulling such a stunt.

About an hour later I spotted them again. This time they were sneaking up behind a captain who was with his wife and two small children. I tried to get his attention to alert him. I whistled and yelled, but he didn't hear me. When the firecrackers went off, he pushed his wife and kids into a doorway and he hit the sidewalk. All this took place in a second or two. His reaction, after realizing what had happened, was different from mine. He spotted the two boys laughing and immediately ran after them. When he caught them, he beat the hell out of them. I don't know if he hurt them seriously or not but I'd be willing to bet that those kids never pulled that stunt on any more combat veterans. There were civilians in the area, but not one intervened.

Meanwhile, I had been raising more hell that I really wanted to, so I looked for a way to get out of Texas. I found it at a six-month training program at a Reconnaissance and Security School in Kansas. Sixty GIs had volunteered from various branches of the service; artillery, transportation, armored, etc. to take this course. We would be promoted to staff sergeants after graduation. I got to Fort Riley just outside of Junction City, Kansas around the first week of January, 1946.

For Riley had been a cavalry post for training horse soldiers in World War I and it was now under the command of a soldier from that war who had risen to the rank of colonel. He was probably about 5'5" tall but he was tough as nails. He ran the camp with an iron fist. Some of the rules he insisted on didn't sit too well with the troops.

[141]

Everyone had to dress the same. That meant that the Infantry guys who wore the bottom of their pants tucked into their combat boots could no longer do that. Other units that wore their caps on the left side of their heads had to change to the right side.

Everyone had to march in formation to class each morning, a distance of half a mile.

No talking while in formation.

Everyone had to fall out for breakfast, hungry or not.

Barracks were to be cleaned every night after class and before anyone could go to town.

Every man took pride in his particular unit and the way they wore their uniforms. I certainly didn't want to wear my pant legs outside of my boot tops. The others wanted to wear their uniforms the way they had always worn them. This led to a "situation" that could have put all 60 of us in the stockade for months—maybe even years.

In our barracks was a GI, Pat Del Vecchio, who was very well versed in what was and what was not allowed in the service. He drew up a petition that started off with, "We the undersigned." You need to know that submitting a petition in the services is considered treason or mutiny or whatever, and carries severe penalties. We may have thought we were immune at this stage of the war or because of what we had been through and the sacrifices we had witnessed. Anyway, here were our requests.

Every man wears his uniform according to his own outfit's regulations. We did not want to be forced to eat if we weren't hungry (plus the fact that the cooks were generally drunk at this early hour). We wanted to walk to class in rout step (no formation), be allowed to talk, and fall into formation just prior to reaching our classroom destination. We also said: no scrubbing the floor or washing windows every night.

When the demands were all listed, all 60 of us signed the petition without hesitation. Pat told us to sign in a "round robin" fashion so the commander would not be able to tell who signed it first. This suggestion probably saved us from getting court-martialed. We thought we would create a little stir, but we certainly weren't ready for the fallout that ensued.

Every one of us had to appear before the colonel and admit or deny that we signed the paper. Standing there before this hard-nosed colonel, as short as he was, was as intimidating an ordeal as I had ever gone through. I was literally shaking in my boots. We all admitted to signing it but we had no knowledge of who signed it first. We were a very nervous group of GIs for a while but it was only a couple of days before the word came down that our "suggestions" were valid. We were free of the regimentation that had plagued us until that time. There was a shake-up in the camp's personnel. The cooks were relieved of their duties and some good cooks were brought in. Our section officer was transferred out of the camp.

Life at the camp became a different experience. We still had to scrub the barracks' floor and wash windows, but only one night a week. It soon became about a five-minute job. Someone would get a bucket of water, throw it down the middle of the floor and each man would swab around his bunk. We sort of "forgot" to do the windows.

One night about four weeks after the petition episode, our new section officer came into our barracks and asked if it was GI night. We told him it was and that we had just finished the job. He looked at the floor and, without saying another word, got up on the edge of someone's cot, put on a white glove, and ran his finger along the top of the molding around the window. "It looks like somebody missed this spot," he said. "How about checking this out before you leave. I'll be back later to check on it."

I don't think a word was spoken by any of us until he walked away, but then we had a lot to say. Those of us who had already changed clothes to go into town changed into fatigues and got ready for a couple of hours of dirty work. The officer did return about two hours later and, instead of checking the molding above the windows, he got up on a footlocker and, with his pocket knife, scraped a lot of crud from the top of the air-conditioning unit. He said, "I think you guys are testing me because I'm new here. I'll be easy on you fellas and give you a chance to make this look good up here." At that moment we knew we wouldn't be going to town that night.

Well, he kept his word and came back after a couple more hours had passed. We were tired but fairly well pleased with the way we had the place looking. This time, what does he do? He gets up on the footlocker again but, instead of checking the top of the air duct, he pulled out a screwdriver and proceeded to take off the little mesh screen in one section. Again, he uses his little pocketknife to scrape up some more crud that had probably been there for 40 years.

I think we all got into bed about 2 or 3 o'clock the next morning. We knew we had met our match. However, our initial dislike for this guy turned into great respect. It turned out that he had been an Infantry officer and been wounded badly enough to have been sent home. He hadn't yelled at us or threatened any further punishment. As it turned out, after another three weeks of cleaning the place up, it took us only a few minutes on GI night to pass his inspection. We even invited him to go with us. He declined, of course.

I almost got a tattoo while I was stationed at Fort Riley. There were about six of us that hung out together when we'd go into town. When we got off the bus, there was a tattoo parlor about one door away. Without fail the owner closed at 5:00 P.M. for a supper break. Even though we hurried we could never get there before 5:00. We'd gather around the window looking at all the possible tattoos one could get. Arthur wanted the one of a snake coiled around his arm. I wanted the black panther's head with the blood red eyes. I think it was six weeks before we finally decided we weren't going to get a tattoo.

From the tattoo shop it was just another block to Ethel's Place. She served beer and sandwiches. Once we got in there, we didn't leave until closing time. Ethel was about 30 or 32 years old and I have never seen a sexier looking woman in all my life. She is why I'm really glad I chose beer over a tattoo. I think every guy that ever saw her asked for a date but she refused them all. There was only one GI that Ethel really went nuts over. He was the same age as we were, 20, but apparently the age difference didn't bother her.

I knew Ernie was a little shy around women, but I didn't think he was that bad. Ethel took matters into her own hands one night and asked him out. She said she'd like to take him to Kansas City, Missouri for a weekend. This idiot refused. Ethel then offered to find a couple of girls for any of his buddies he wanted to take along. Still he said no, even though we were all yelling at him to accept her offer. Ethel then offered Ernie the use of her Cadillac convertible while he was stationed in Fort Riley. I guess he liked cars better than "older" women because he accepted that offer. However, he got so much flak from his buddies that he quit using it. As far as I know Ethel never dated any of the guys I knew.

We finished our training and were given 30-day furloughs. After mine, I had to report back to Camp Carson in Colorado Springs where I was to talk about my future. I was asked to re-enlist and make the Army my career. The recruiter told me I could retire at the early age of 38 with 20 years in the service and get a nice pension. I was only 20 years old and thought I'd be an old man when I got out. I told him I might consider re-upping for three years because I wanted to see more of the world and there weren't any wars going on.

When I said I wanted to be transferred to any outfit but an infantry one, I was told that would be just about impossible. He mentioned the fact that the 10th Mountain Division had some openings I might be interested in. I asked him what they were and he said, "Right now, they are in upstate Washington, testing cold-weather gear." I told him I had just spent one

[147]

winter out in a snow-covered foxhole, freezing my butt off. Then I had no choice, but I certainly wasn't going to volunteer to do that again.

I took my discharge option and had to return to Camp Devens in Massachusetts where it all started a couple of years before. In the long run, I was glad I did take the discharge because the 2nd Division was the first unit sent to Korea when the war started four years later. I felt that I made it through one war but I doubted I would have survived another being in the Infantry.

The guys I used to hang out with had survived the war, too, and we all got together to celebrate. The best way, we decided, was to take advantage of the 52-20 club--$20 a week from Uncle Sam for 52 weeks to give us a chance to settle in and find work. Four of us spent the summer at Hampton Beach, New Hampshire in a cabin we rented for $16 a week. We had one fantastic time; swimming, lying out on the beach, meeting girls.

While I had heard about guys suffering terrible nightmares after the war, I was sleeping fine at this point. I was unaware, however, that deep in my subconscious the sights and sounds of war were still with me. It became clear one day when the four of us were near a construction site on the beach and some wires supporting a large piece of equipment snapped. The sound was exactly like a bullet ricocheting.

Without a second's hesitation, I flattened out on the beach. My buddies, who had never been shot at or knew the sound of a bullet ricocheting, were mystified and asked me what had happened. I wasn't going to tell them the real reason I hit the sand so I told them I was practicing in case anybody was shooting at me. They called me crazy and that was the end of that.

After that summer ended we came back home and we all got jobs working at the Massachusetts Institute of Technology. We worked together for several years, while going to night school to get our degrees. Eventually, our different interests took us on different paths. But three of us are alive today and we keep in contact. For me, it's been an interesting life full of the usual ups and downs and I feel blessed to have survived for so long.

Occasionally, I think of those days on the front lines and the great guys I met who never made it back. I may not remember all the names but I can still see their faces. After a heavy firefight one time, I spoke with a chaplain who said: "Son, when things are really bad, just remember, that this, too, shall pass." As simple a piece of advice as it was, it has helped me many times over the years. After surviving front-line duty and its horrors, I had the idea that anything from here on out would be a piece of cake. Things have not always been a piece of cake but at least I could face them, and they did pass.

[149]

EPILOGUE

My great appreciation goes to the GIs who fought alongside me, and especially to those soldiers who fought in more extreme and difficult situations than I did. I didn't have to worry about jungle warfare, malaria, shortages of warm clothes in freezing weather, death marches, imprisonment or daily torture. My enemy all wore uniforms and the civilians pretty much stayed out of our way. And, that is important. When you have to face soldiers who do not wear uniforms, how are you going to distinguish them from the civilians who are trying to kill you? You don't want to kill innocents but when your life is the price you pay for a mistake, then you do what you must.

I will grant you that atrocities are committed by any country that goes to war. But until you've been in the position of having to pull a trigger when your life is on the line, it's best not to make any judgment calls about morality.

Even though I came close to being killed several times, I would do it all over if I had to. I wouldn't *want to* but I love this country. We can complain and bitch about various things the government has done—and I have done my share—but I still wouldn't want to live anywhere else. At least I have the privilege of free speech and the freedom to go and come as I please. That is not possible in many countries today.

PHOTOS

Stan with his wife, Chat

High School Graduation 1943

Stan & Al Stucki

Al was the interpreter for Stan's unit

Stan, Charlie & Carl

At Nuremberg

A German POW made this sketch of Stan in 1945

Pat DelVecchio & Stan

Del Vecchio, the "barracks lawyer"

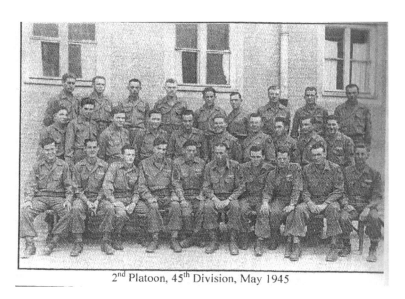

2nd Platoon, 45th Division, May 1945

Stan is in the second row, sixth from the left

Made in the USA
Middletown, DE
26 November 2014